MIDSTREAM

BOOKS BY
REYNOLDS PRICE

MIDSTREAM   2012
ARDENT SPIRITS   2009
LETTER TO A GODCHILD   2006
THE GOOD PRIEST'S SON   2005
A SERIOUS WAY OF WONDERING   2003
NOBLE NORFLEET   2002
FEASTING THE HEART   2000
A PERFECT FRIEND   2000
LETTER TO A MAN IN THE FIRE   1999
LEARNING A TRADE   1998
ROXANNA SLADE   1998
THE COLLECTED POEMS   1997
THREE GOSPELS   1996
THE PROMISE OF REST   1995
A WHOLE NEW LIFE   1994
THE COLLECTED STORIES   1993
FULL MOON   1993
BLUE CALHOUN   1992
THE FORESEEABLE FUTURE   1991
NEW MUSIC   1990
THE USE OF FIRE   1990
THE TONGUES OF ANGELS   1990
CLEAR PICTURES   1989
GOOD HEARTS   1988
A COMMON ROOM   1987
THE LAWS OF ICE   1986
KATE VAIDEN   1986
PRIVATE CONTENTMENT   1984
VITAL PROVISIONS   1982
THE SOURCE OF LIGHT   1981
A PALPABLE GOD   1978
EARLY DARK   1977
THE SURFACE OF EARTH   1975
THINGS THEMSELVES   1972
PERMANENT ERRORS   1970
LOVE AND WORK   1968
A GENEROUS MAN   1966
THE NAMES AND FACES OF HEROES   1963
A LONG AND HAPPY LIFE   1962

REYNOLDS PRICE

MIDSTREAM

AN UNFINISHED MEMOIR

SCRIBNER

NEW YORK   LONDON   TORONTO   SYDNEY   NEW DELHI

SCRIBNER
A Division of Simon & Schuster, Inc.
1230 Avenue of the Americas
New York, NY 10020

First Scribner hardcover edition May 2012

SCRIBNER and design are registered trademarks of The Gale Group, Inc.,
used under license by Simon & Schuster, Inc., the publisher of this work.

For information about special discounts for bulk purchases,
please contact Simon & Schuster Special Sales at 1-866-506-1949
or business@simonandschuster.com.

The Simon & Schuster Speakers Bureau can bring authors to your live event.
For more information or to book an event, contact the Simon & Schuster Speakers
Bureau at 1-866-248-3049 or visit our website at www.simonspeakers.com.

Manufactured in the United States of America

1 3 5 7 9 10 8 6 4 2

ISBN 978-1-4391-8349-6
ISBN 978-1-4391-8355-7 (ebook)

PHOTO CREDITS

pp. 16, 40, 48, 100, and 104: Photographs courtesy of the Reynolds Price Papers,
David M. Rubenstein Rare Book & Manuscript Library, Duke University; p. 90:
Photograph of American composer Samuel Barber © Bettmann/Corbis

CONTENTS

FOREWORD

It was the fall of 1958, and I was registering for freshman English in the Duke University gymnasium. But the instructor wasn't sure that she could fit me into her class. She sat frowning down at my card till the man sitting next to her said, "What's the problem?" and reached over to take it from her. He was young and distinctly exotic-looking, at least to a North Carolina girl who had never been anywhere. His hair was a deep, dense black, and one of his curls had sprung away from the rest to dangle over his forehead.

"Oh, well," he said after a moment, "I'll take her."

And that is how I met the teacher of my life.

My class was the first that Reynolds Price ever taught, but you never would have guessed it. From day one he was a natural: easygoing, humorous, relaxed. He had a way of implying that we were all in this together—that if a student came up with a striking insight, it was occasion for every last one of us to rejoice. "You're *good* at this, aren't you?" he said once to a girl who had offered a particularly astute interpretation of a poem. I still remember the surprise and dawning pleasure that showed in her face, and I'll bet she remembers, too.

He wasn't spendthrift with his praise, though. For those of us who came from small-town high schools, where we were routinely made much of, there was something shocking and yet oddly exhilarating in his forthright "You went wrong, here." No patronizing pats on the head from Reynolds! At the end of my freshman year I wrote a story about a poverty-stricken black woman lying in a hospital bed; she looked at her hands on top of the sheet and they reminded her of an India-ink drawing. "That would not happen," Reynolds said firmly. "A thing like an India-ink drawing wouldn't cross that woman's mind." He was right, of course. I recognized it with a feeling something like relief. You could say that it was a matter of respect: he took us seriously enough to tell us the truth.

Most important, at least when it came to the composition part of the class, was his gift for inspiration. He was a budding writer, as it turned out. (A writer! We were in awe.) His short stories were just beginning to be published, and sometimes he read us one aloud, sitting tailor-fashion on top of his desk and rolling out each word in his thunderously vibrant voice. All at once, *we* wanted to write. We could barely sit still in our chairs; we wanted to rush back to our rooms that very minute and create something as mesmerizing and seemingly effortless as what he was reading to us.

During my sophomore year he was working on his first novel, *A Long and Happy Life*. Chapter one appeared in the magazine *Encounter*, and he arrived in my dormitory lobby with a signed reprint—an act of kindness that takes my breath away to this day. I started reading it the instant he left, and I will never forget the impact of that first long, sinuous sentence where Wesley Beavers careens his motorcycle in and out of a funeral procession with Rosacoke Mustian pressed against his back.

Small wonder that for the creative writing class he taught the year after that, all of us turned in stories that sounded like a combination of Reynolds Price and J. D. Salinger. (Salinger was very big just then.) Not that Reynolds *asked* to be imitated; he showed a clear appreciation for any sign of differentness in his students. But

we were all so starstruck, and besides, there was something uncannily contagious about his style. Spend enough time in his company
and you'd end up talking like him, even—using phrases like "God's
green earth," one of his favorites. Another professor once wrote me
a note saying he felt my work "would have a lot more value if there
were a little less Price in it." He had a point. (You notice I've memo-
rized his words.)

Hard to resist Reynolds's influence, though. Just look at him fly-
ing across the campus, curls bouncing, dark eyes flashing, and a
black cape (I swear it) flaring out behind him. Actually he never
owned a black cape; he told me that, years later. He said it was a
navy jacket, just tossed over his shoulders. But still, he was wearing
a *virtual* cape, if you know what I mean. He was an exclamation
point in a landscape of mostly declarative sentences. He lived in
a house-trailer out in the woods; he invited us to come there and
drink smoky-tasting tea in handmade mugs. Speaking with a trace
of an English accent from his recent studies at Oxford (for he had
a genius for unintentional mimicry, which he said could become
a curse in certain situations), he told us funny, affectionate tales
about his childhood in backwater Macon. Most of us came from
Macons of our own; we were astonished to hear that they were fit
subjects for storytelling. All over again, inspiration hit. Let us out of
there! We had to get back to our rooms and start writing.

Add to this the presence of William Blackburn, another wonderful writing teacher who had taught Reynolds himself, and you see
why Duke University turned out so many writers in those days. Dr.
Blackburn's signature method was the anguished groan he would
utter as we read one of our clumsier sentences aloud—a nice coun-
terpoint to Reynolds's ebullience.

During my last year at Duke, Reynolds told me that he'd arranged
for me to be represented by his agent, Diarmuid Russell. (This was a

pass-it-on kind of favor, because Eudora Welty had made the same arrangement for Reynolds a few years before, after she visited Duke and read Reynolds's undergraduate work.) At the time, I had no idea what an enormous gift I'd been given. I wasn't even sure what an agent did, to be honest. I thanked Reynolds politely and then forgot all about it till much later, when I had a novel to peddle and I thought, "Wait! Isn't this something I could ask that agent about?"

But anyhow, I graduated and left Duke behind, at the same time that Reynolds left for a second stay in England. It would be more than thirteen years before I saw him again.

In 1974, he telephoned to invite me to Duke for a week of readings and workshops. We sent letters back and forth about the arrangements, but not till he met my plane (waiting all windswept on the tarmac, the way people could do in those days) did I know for sure that he hadn't lost his old joyousness. There were a few threads of white in his hair now, but his face was as round and cherubic as ever, and I felt as I observed him over the course of the week that he was like a favorite child in a family of doting relatives. He held court expansively on the stage of the Duke auditorium; he set up ripples of alertness and laughter when he stepped into other instructors' writing classes. Driving into a service station to fill his tank, he was met by a mechanic cowering comically and covering his head—a reference to the fact that the week before, Reynolds had absentmindedly driven off with the gas nozzle still hooked to his car. Visiting a men's clothing store, he was teased by the salesclerks for faithfully attending every half-price sale but in the end choosing the classier, nonsale merchandise. Restaurant meals with him were like little cocktail parties; people stopped by our table to talk, and he listened gravely to each of them and then after they left he told us their stories, quoting dialogue word for word in exactly their own intonations.

We kept in closer touch, after that. He came to Baltimore a few times; he met my husband and my children; every so often we wrote to each other. By then he must have been corresponding with dozens of his ex-students; he had so many of them, and they'd done so well. He told me once that we were all his children, but what felt like even more of an honor was when he called us his friends. "Your old friend," he would refer to himself in his letters, and sometimes he would depart from his usual breezy tone to reveal something serious—admitting once, for instance, that he had never found the same deep satisfaction in teaching that William Blackburn had. That surprised me. Was it because it came so easily to him that he didn't value his own accomplishments?

He wrote after reading one of my books that he wished my novels would start featuring more intellectual characters; also (as a kind of afterthought) that I should smile in my jacket photos. He reported on his work, on his travels, and then eventually, shockingly, on the paralysis that developed after his spinal surgery. He came to visit again, this time in a wheelchair and with an attendant to help him navigate our steps, but he was his usual cheery self, and I remember how he and my husband egged each other on, the two of them possessing the same irrepressible high spirits.

I wonder, now, if those of us who loved Reynolds did him a disservice in taking those high spirits at face value. I think of the time I returned to Durham to research a profile of him before the publication of *Kate Vaiden*. After demonstrating his brand-new "Rolls Royce of a wheelchair," as he called it, executing a few fancy spins around his living room, he suddenly grew serious. "But when you write about this," he said, "I hope you won't minimize things. This is *hard*. The pain I'm in would make you scream if you had to feel it for even a second. I hope you won't gloss that over."

No, I said, I wouldn't do that. But I felt chastised, in a way, because up till then I had been laughing at his antics. He had been so convincing, larking about in his wheelchair; I had almost seen that cape of his flaring out behind him.

I knew he had his dark times. Some of them he'd referred to in his memoirs—particularly the period just after his surgery when the paralysis began to set in. And once, he'd said straight out that he was subject to depression. Yet he always gave me the sense that he was a naturally happy man—one of the happiest I've known. Besides, look at how the subject of depression had come up: he'd brandished a life-sized woman's leg made of chocolate (a joke birthday gift, evidently) and told me, with some glee, that he chipped off a chunk every evening as "self-medication," since the rumor was that dark chocolate was just as good as Prozac. And I had laughed, of course.

He was much too good at making me laugh.

Years after that visit, when my husband was dealing with the lymphoma that eventually led to his death, Reynolds sent me an encouraging letter. He ended it with an Emily Dickinson poem that he said he'd only just discovered:

> *There is a strength in proving that it can be borne*
> *Although it tear—*
> *What are the sinews of such cordage for*
> *Except to bear*
> *The ship might be of satin had it not to fight—*
> *The walk on seas requires cedar Feet*

"Seems serviceable," was his comment, "for numerous moments of any adult's life."

Yes, certainly. But most especially for Reynolds Price's life.

—Anne Tyler
Baltimore, Maryland

EDITOR'S NOTE
ON THE TEXT

WHEN REYNOLDS PRICE DIED in January 2011, he left behind the unfinished (and unedited) manuscript of *Midstream*. As his brother, William Price, notes in his Afterword, Reynolds intended to write a book of some 350 manuscript pages, of which he completed only 208. A hard copy of these pages found in Reynolds's home in North Carolina contained numerous handwritten revisions and notations. Making use of his extensive archive of correspondence with Reynolds during the period this memoir describes, the writer Wallace Kaufman, a former student and longtime friend, typed Reynolds's handwritten revisions into the final manuscript and verified as many details as possible. In a few cases, where Reynolds's letters contradict or clarify portions of the original manuscript, Kaufman—in collaboration with William Price and a Scribner editor—altered the manuscript using Reynolds's original wording from his letters. Reynolds also left a list of photographs he wanted to include in *Midstream*. William Price has sought them out and written the captions that appear here. The book also underwent Scribner's standard editing and copyediting procedures by a team who have worked on several of Reynolds's books—with all edits reviewed by William Price. The end result is a more complete text, still fully written by Reynolds Price.

MIDSTREAM

PREFACE

IN THE FIRST three volumes of memoir, I covered some five decades of my life. *Clear Pictures* began at my birth in 1933. *Ardent Spirits* follows with sailing to England in the summer of 1955 for three years of graduate study at Oxford, moves through my return to teach at Duke University, and closes with my first novel being prepared for publication as I sail for a fourth year at Oxford in July 1961. (A briefer volume, *A Whole New Life*, describes a hard passage through spinal cancer and paraplegia. Covering some four years beginning in 1984, it concludes at an age at which many men sense their mortality as a hard bite at the back of the neck. It sees me through that long ordeal to the partial healing that allowed me to continue writing and teaching.)

I'm now in my late seventies; and with this present volume— *Midstream*—I've studied nearly half my conscious life. It begins immediately after the end of *Ardent Spirits*. Docked once more in Southampton, England, I'm facing north for a fourth year in Oxford, where I'm expecting high degrees of pleasure (my hopes will not be entirely daunted). This time in England I'd have no academic duties but for almost a year would seek renewed pleasure with friends and a former lover, and also await the publication of my first novel. Then I returned to my home in North Carolina to continue teaching and writing more fiction while caring for my mother through an initially mysterious illness that led to her death. After she was gone, our family grief was met by a disorderly response on my own part—a search for love by a man in his mid-thirties who was faced by not only his mother's death but also his brother's departure for war in Vietnam. It seemed an inescapable reality that my small family—one that had meant a great deal to me—had all but disappeared.

In these four volumes I have avoided only the events which belong most intimately to others still living. In this present work I've been helped by my family's chief historian—my brother, Will Price, who's taken time from his many years of work in American history to search out answers to questions I set before him as my own curiosity coiled and reopened on itself. He claims that he's enjoyed the time he's spent; I've more than enjoyed the answers he's found and the time we've spent in regret and laughter. Above all, I thank him for the help he's given his older brother—our first job together. May other chances come our way.

*"What you maybe don't know is that I always go into a decline
at times like this—saying to myself that surely it would be far easier
just to sit still and forget the whole thing, but then I think
of a fourth consecutive year in Durham and plow on."*
—Reynolds Price, in a letter
to Wallace Kaufman, July 8, 1961

AFTER DEBARKING FROM the *Queen Mary* and clearing customs on the Southampton dock by ten in the morning, I leapt aboard a train for Oxford with my small borrowed trunk and one suitcase. In the three years since I was last in England, British Railways had surely not upgraded the third-class car I rode in—musty gray upholstery and a good deal of empty space. Nonetheless I reached my destination—Merton College's thirteenth-century entrance lodge—just in time to collide with my tall old teacher and friend Nevill Coghill. He swept me up to join him for lunch in the Senior Common Room. The new scout for the rooms on my staircase, one of the several men that served the "young gentlemen" in the still all-male colleges, carried my bags along to my former rooms in the ancient Mob Quad—the same two rooms with an overstuffed sofa and chairs (that suggested ancient Rome more than medieval Britain) and windows on the college chestnut tree and Christ Church Meadow with its cows and football-playing schoolboys. Oxford was, mostly, unchanged. There had been a lot of cleaning and refacing of college buildings—the coal-black Virgin on Merton Chapel turned out on washing to be very beautiful—but my old rooms seemed quite unchanged and full.

In the SCR it was a welcome surprise to find my old love Matyas already seated at the table. He'd walked over from his own college on the chance that I might have arrived by then, and here now I was (the trains mostly ran on time). Still his dashing self, though a little weary around the eyes, Matyas beamed his expected magnetism; but slight signs suggested that his intervening trips to his family home in Eastern Europe had saddened him appreciably (and in what ways did he see that I'd likewise changed after my first three years of teaching at Duke?). Well, Common Room table was hardly a place for private talk between us, but other talk there was aplenty—and in quantity and quality as I'd hoped.

In a matter of minutes then, I was enveloped in what I'd anticipated so strongly (though my student friends were gone)—the compelling but unpretentious melding of mind in mature male voices. Not that I'd been entirely deprived of good talk in America. Lately in Macon, Warrenton, Raleigh, Durham, New York, and a few other places, I'd felt delighted and instructed more than a few times by a wide spectrum of several brands of good talk. But in no other place had I sat with others as enthusiastically devoted as these few men round a long broad table to genuine discourse. In addition to weeks in my old rooms again, I'd been made a member of the Senior Common Room; so with any luck at all, I'd just commenced a fourth year of this.

My main hope lay in Matyas though, a don from Eastern Europe with whom—in my last visit to England—I'd experienced an intense romance, one that I thought had at least some amount of love on each side as well as sexual contact of a highly exciting new kind. In days when few dons traveled to the States (and none seemed to emigrate, as hundreds do now), we'd kept our mutual awareness alive by my gift for long-distance longing, by frequent letters, and my own hell-bent intention to meet back here as soon as my slim funds would permit.

After lunch Nevill suggested a walk round Christ Church Meadow, so Matyas and I joined him under a sky that by then was brilliantly clear and hot for June. Even the regulation loud red geraniums were lusher than I remembered; and as we passed those on the window ledges of student rooms in the Christ Church Meadow building, Nevill said "It *would* seem a sizable pity, wouldn't it?"

I asked "What would?"

With a wide wave of his huge right hand, he said "Just to end it now, with all this around us."

In five days on the ocean, I hadn't quite heard that the Western powers and the Soviets were once again shaking their hydrogen bombs at one another over the still divided city of Berlin.

Refusing for now to cloud the day, I remarked that such crises had been far from rare in the reign of Khrushchev, but Nevill said that this one somehow felt especially ominous.

Matyas laconically agreed. Since the Soviets ran the Nazis out of his homeland and seized all power there, he knew a good deal about them.

Nevill had fought in the trenches of World War I, but now he grinned. "Wars tend to begin in gorgeous weather. I remember 1914 clear as now."

He'd lent a sudden chill to our walk, and as we finished one round of the Meadow, Matyas peeled off for an afternoon appointment, arranging that he and I would dine that night in his rooms in his own college. It was I who'd introduced Matyas to Nevill back in the spring of 1958; and I knew from our letters that, since Matyas often dined in Merton—where he had a few pupils—he'd come to enjoy Nevill's company. As he walked away then, Nevill and I stood for ten seconds and watched his departure through the War Memorial Gardens and out through the tall Meadow gates. We didn't say as much, but I know we were silently granting Matyas's compelling physical power.

When he was finally out of sight, Nevill turned to me and said "Ah, Matyas, yes. I know he's expected you." If the older man knew more than that, he kept his own counsel.

Nevill had bought a small car in my absence; and after I'd had my customary postlunch nap and unpacked a little, he drove the two of us out to Thame for tea. Like many occupants of sun-deprived countries, he was capitalizing on the brightness of the day. The village itself was of no special interest to me; but in my old car trips to London, I'd always craned, when passing through the surroundings of Thame, to discover the rambling medieval house which Laurence Olivier and Vivien Leigh (the acting Oliviers) had occupied for decades. Despite the reports of the coming collapse of their long marriage, they were the chief Britons who still aroused celebrity feeling in me (and had done so since I first saw her in *Gone With the Wind* in 1939 and the two of them in *That Hamilton Woman* a little later); and I was hoping to see each of them onstage before the year ended.

Still, Nevill's good talk—and his unintrusive questions about my life—held me later than I'd planned. Back at Merton then in early evening, I raced to the spanking-new showers in my old scout's pantry on the ground floor of Mob 2 and availed myself of actual liberally streaming warm water. When a few college members came in to shower near me, I was reminded of another trait of the local times. Once dry, these young gents each resumed the underpants he'd worn to the shower. There was still no sign of the American middle-class obsession with clean laundry against clean skin. Pristine myself, though, I turned up at seven at the unshut outer door of Matyas's new rooms in his across-town college.

The outer door was called an oak. And this oak had a special meaning for me. More than a few times three years ago, Matyas had shut us in behind his oak—the universal Oxford sign that no one was to knock or, in any other way short of fire or civil mayhem, disturb the occupant. I knocked on the inner door; and it took Matyas at least two minutes to answer, a delay so unusual that I wondered if he had someone else with him. When I entered, however, we embraced at last—a cooler greeting than I'd expected. Matyas indicated a handsome chair he'd just got in London, then stepped aside to pour us white wine. While he was apart I looked round the pleasantly large sitting room, a good deal brighter than his former quarters across the quad.

When he rejoined me, he noted my interest and told me, at unnecessary length, the history of various new objects (I didn't ask whether he or the college had paid for the elegant furniture).

Before we could turn to anything more interesting, Matyas told me that—if it was all the same with me—we'd eat in his rooms and not go out.

"All the finer," I said.

Then he came to his point. First, he gave the downcast laugh that, with him, mostly signaled bad news. Then he moved on in an accent that had decidedly thickened in the trips he'd made to Eastern Europe since getting his British citizenship at the time of our last meeting—"Rey-nolds, there is just one important thing."

His long pause enforced a slow "Yes?" from me. I felt what I guessed a student might have felt as he finished reading a mediocre essay to this demanding tutor. Whatever was coming, the fault was mine.

"Lately I've met a charming young woman, almost my age. She's also not British, she lives in London, and I suspect that we're growing closer."

No such relation had been mentioned in his recent letters; and I was more than surprised, though I strained to conceal it.

As soon as he led me to the long new teak table, he began to serve dinner. I recall only that we began with mushrooms *à la grecque*, a first for me and impressive, and that Matyas talked on and on with only occasional one-word responses from me. Not even the most ardently dedicated Gatekeeper of Western Morals could have sat and silently watched us for that first half hour and left with any suspicion that, three years ago, we'd been fervent lovers through a spring and early summer—unreserved possessors of one another's bodies—and that I, at least, had sensed something durable under way in the interim.

Well into the main course, Matyas had reached what he plainly felt I'd understand as his central news—he wasn't now planning to resume our old relations while he was hoping this new connection was going to work (whatever *work* would mean).

More than ever, I felt how much older than me he apparently felt; or maybe now I was the don and he the frantic student. What I felt though was far more like a pluperfect fool, a fool who might be shown the door shortly. But I sat on, through salad and dessert, and heard a good deal that the regular letters of three years had omitted— omissions that I had not suspected in my reckless craving.

Matyas had experienced more than several intervening affairs here, in London, and on the continent. Eventually all his philandering (as he saw it and he'd after all begun life as a devout Catholic boy) had resulted in degrees of futility and self-loathing that led him—when he met the young woman he'd mentioned—to experiment with the possibility of a long-term heterosexual union. Something, yes, that might become a marriage with a home and children—an all but universal reality that he hadn't experienced since he was sixteen.

After four courses of such revelations, I'd begun to feel fed up with more than a lesson in my sustained foolishness. For the first time in my life apparently, I'd agreed to be lied to. To be sure, there'd been one hard letter that virtually accused me of having led him back astray (at a time when he was in his mid-thirties). Still I couldn't see why he let me plan this costly fourth year while I leaned like a dope, approaching thirty, on the expectation of something I longed to continue. Even more than my foolishness, on the spot I learned how a great many men—and women, no doubt—find it all but impossible to tell a close friend a disappointing truth.

By late evening then I'd expressed no anger, but Matyas must have seen my severe disappointment. Well, at least he'd disillusioned me on the night of my arrival. And surely he took no pleasure in the news—or was there a brassy ring of cruelty in the air? I couldn't believe that. Whatever, I began to say a calm enough good night. Then Matyas dropped what was, by then, the heaviest shoe of the evening. Would I be so good as to meet with his new friend very soon and discuss with her—one on one—the nature of my old relation with him, explaining as much as I could of his sexual complexities?

I'd like to think I roared with laughter. I didn't. But I know I said a plain "Not a chance. Not a chance on Earth." I allowed I'd be interested in meeting her, but I wouldn't enliven a private meeting with personal secrets.

Back in my rooms twenty minutes later, I partly unpacked—no one to invite me for a late-night drink, no one else, it seemed, in the entire quad. Yet the ancient space, home to almost seven centuries of young men's miseries and elations, was a kind of harbor after the bright and startling day—no nuclear weapons had exploded; and I'd already begun to feel the rising (round my core) of a toughness inherited from both my parents. I was shocked by Matyas's deceit,

humiliated in my childish blindness, but hardly devastated. I had a
novel of which I was proud coming slowly down the production line
for simultaneous publication in the States and in Britain; and I was
in a city and nation populated with surely reliable friends, none of
whom I'd armed with the weapons to attack me.

I've spoken, just above, of Matyas's deceit. How wrong was that?
Was it deceit or only a continuation of the frightened confusion I
thought I'd detected when we parted in a London hotel in '58—a
scared aging boy, caught by the Nazis in '45, imprisoned by them
and then separated from his family for more than a decade, alone in
a country of absolute strangers till he'd wrung out a thoroughly honorable life from two of the world's great universities by sheer intelligence, a handsome head, and a deep-voiced charm? Before I could
convince myself I knew a true answer, the long day overwhelmed
me; and I slept again on the still-spiny straw mattress atop a wood
bed that might well have borne more than a thousand men; each
at least as alone as I and deprived of the touch of another human
body (though in medieval Oxford, students often slept two or more
to a bed).

I'd kept no journal of my first three years at Oxford; but as soon as
I arrived for my fourth, I went to the nearby lane called the Turl and
in a stationer's I bought a small blank book with lined pages and
began to keep, not quite a journal but a daily calendar. The habit
proved to be that I didn't write more than a page about any day of
the year; and in the face of an unusual quiet, I could write the barest
minimum of lines. It turned out that I almost always related events
without comment, except on surprising occasions worth remembering. Amazingly I managed to write at least a few words about every
day of those months; and I've now reread each page, for the first
time in forty-odd years.

I felt, in my prior memoir *Ardent Spirits*, that there'd be some point in relating the events, thoughts, and feelings of my first stint at Oxford. As the final student years of my life, they were of crucial importance in defining who I then was and who I'd be, for better or worse, through the remainder of my life—especially who I'd be as a novelist, poet, playwright, essayist, and teacher. So the fourth year was hardly going to prove unimportant for me—how could it? It was, maybe above all, the last year of my twenties. I'd be twenty-nine when I headed back to the States; and I've often noted that white middle-class men, with a good deal of formal education, see their thirtieth birthday as an especially significant, even a depressing, milestone.

The most ominous reality of age thirty is likely to be realization that *This is it. I'm now the person I'm likely to be—barring mental or physical accident—from here to the end. The choices I've made, especially the choice of a career (and the choice of a mate or partner), are likely to endure. So it's* Like It or Lump It *for some fifty years more; and what can* Lump It *consist of—a descent into drink or drugs, homeless wandering, or eventual suicide?*

I'd discussed the age-thirty hurdle with several of my slightly older teaching colleagues before I returned to Oxford, so I was aware of my renewed English time as a particularly loaded event. And while I don't recall taking special care, with that hurdle in mind just down the road, I also knew that my first book would be published before I reached thirty. If the novel met with any degree of success, wouldn't life simplify or improve? Or would it? Would a sizable success also be a torpedo? In the frequent solitary hours of the fourth year, I gave a fair amount of thought to such questions—hardly unrealistic concerns in the face of what was rapidly coming down the road toward me, ready or not.

Despite the survival of my diary notes, I won't describe the year in anything resembling detail—and once and for all, I've already described their single real sadness. I can see from here that they were mainly a stretch of pleasure with friends. I doubt that I learned a third of what I'd learned in my first Oxford stint, but I may well have laughed a good deal more—I certainly rested more and I lavishly rewarded myself for the previous three years of double-barreled hard work of writing and teaching. Not to mention the continued, though unintended, degree of lone celibacy. I'll concentrate then on what was most important in friendship and work and hope to organize those matters as economically as truth allows.

Five days after landing I set off on serious water again. I was bound for my friend Michael Jordan's wedding to Vanja Hultgren in Stockholm. On the afternoon of July 23 in London I met Colin Willmott, an artist, who had been Mike's roommate in Washington, D.C. where Mike worked for the World Bank and Colin for a British engineering firm. We took the boat train to the east coast at Harwich. From there we sailed before dark in a first-class cabin on the *Kronprinz Frederick,* and we landed at Esbjerg in Denmark at midday on the twenty-fourth. Then we boarded a train for Copenhagen where we spent an hour wandering through the decorous pleasures of the central amusement park, Tivoli. I'd been there with Michael in 1956, and now I even got a second glimpse of its famous flea circus, though the Ben-Hur chariot race (entirely run by fleas) had gone to a well-earned rest with its well-trained Siphonaptera.

Then we spent a miserable night on the train toward Stockholm. Colin was more amused than I by our compartment mates—five plump pre-adolescent Swedish girl scouts who slept barely a wink, but when they did Colin noted their "unladylike positions" and uniformly blue knickers. Plagued as they apparently were by universal bladder infections, they left for the john one by one every five minutes through the sleepless dark and always returned with high giggles and loud complaints. Still we reached Stockholm alive eleven hours later (my second visit to that stately city) and were met at the station by a cheerful Mike and Vanja, not yet exhausted by multiple prenuptial celebrations, another of which they soon rushed off to attend.

Travel-worn as Colin and I were, we paused near the station for real barbershop shaves. It was to be my single lifetime experience with a gleaming straight razor in the hands of another human being scraping my jugular for a long quarter hour. Owner of the lavish black beard that I then was, I'm glad to concede to the barber that he left me so well shorn that I didn't need another shave for two days. Then we rambled through the spotless but likable alleys of the old town, till at last we got access to a borrowed apartment arranged by Colin. We both felt the need of a short nap before dinner and lay down at 6:30 p.m.—to wake exactly twelve hours later.

In the next two days, we joined Mike and Vanja in various pleasures and chores—a trip to see the suburban Markuskyrkan where the marriage would occur. Then there were shopping and dining jaunts—Mike's mother, Anne Jordan—known to us as "Win"—had now arrived plus another of their Washington friends, a droll Frenchman our age named François. On the evening of the twenty-eighth, we three friends of the groom took him and his mother to dinner in Skansen, another central Scandinavian amusement park. For the occasion, Mike had picked a spacious airy restaurant overlooking the city; and Colin, François, and I proceeded to a lavish celebration—we each drank five generous shots of schnapps. It produced only jolliness. Eventually, we wandered around all the tables, co-opting the prevailing décor which consisted of small flags from a great many nations (all the other guests cooperated smilingly, and the management were smilingly tolerant). Given our obvious good cheer, we wound up with dozens of flags at our own table.

Further schnapps were provided *gratis* by amused other diners; and down our hatches they all promptly went. Toward the end of our meal, even I could see that both Colin and François were considerably more hardened to the bracing substance than I. Mike had signed off a few glasses earlier; and by the time he left at near midnight to take his mother to her room, I was distinctly looped.

Next the three of us attempted to enter a lively dance hall slightly downhill in Skansen and were refused by two unsmiling doormen. They said we were too late, but our lively condition was surely the cause. In any case just as we turned away from the entrance, I was monumentally ill in the adjacent shrubbery. Undeterred, Colin and François were determined to push on with further night life; but at my earnest petition, we hustled into a taxi and the two friends returned me to the borrowed apartment and proceeded to undress me for bed (soused for only the second time in my life, I was singing all the while). Then they left me unconscious.

Thank God, I woke at six—it was the wedding day; and I vaguely realized I had a good deal to do, chiefly repair work on my trousers and shoes. I managed to wash the shoes and the pants cuffs, which I successfully pressed with an iron I found in the kitchen. By the time Colin woke and François joined us at ten, we were all ready for a large breakfast before taking the subway to the church. By the time we surfaced into a bright morning, we all confessed to splitting headaches; and Colin led us into a ladies' shop where the helpful female attendants gave us aspirin which braced us for the simple ceremony.

I sat with Colin in the second row. The wedding itself was absolutely simple in a fine bare modern church with Bach beforehand. There were recognizable Protestant hymns (in Swedish to be sure); and clear glass windows opening on slender white birches taller than the church, the windowpanes so clear I might well have levitated, slid through them, and vanished on down into the woods. I even thought I might prefer that escape to sitting here, but of course I failed to seize the chance, so I sat on loyally to witness the whole rite. The ceremony ended with the hymn "Fairest Lord Jesus, Ruler of All Nature," which, even in Swedish, is about the most beautiful of all. It had been lean and quick in its Lutheran way: a way which, for all I knew there in St. Mark's Church, might have taken this man and woman to parallel graves, bowed down with life's weight some sixty years from now.

I won't swear to it from this late point; but in memory at least this marriage of Michael, the first great love of my life, caused me no enduring pain; and at the end I was almost glad to have stayed to see it—one more thing I'd borne without a spooked escape. Then members of Vanja's large and astonishingly handsome young family drove us all out to the village hall in Alta for an enormous midday meal—one which called to mind so many other such outdoor whistle-stop celebrations in nineteenth-century novels—admirable chances when lavish food, drink, and a day's human closeness made their often repeated effort to assert that the vows of love and loyalty would endure as long as one of the stout wood tables round which everyone sat.

We went on till, at five, we waved the knockout-beautiful bride and groom away. Then Colin and I and Mike's mother dined again at a good restaurant late in the evening back in the city. Though my male friends planned further late hijinks, I caved in gladly and headed back to bed, as full of food as I was of mixed emotions. An attempt at honest reconstruction, from four decades later, might go like this. In the time I'd known Vanja, I'd learned to like her forthright feelings and her readiness to laugh. And since I'd always known Mike would marry someone before he reached thirty, she seemed to me a good choice. Strangely again, I felt secure in the

Michael Jordan, Reynolds's most cherished and enduring friend in a lifetime filled with friends, on Michael's wedding day in Stockholm in the summer of 1961. Reynolds would dedicate two of his novels to Mike — *A Long and Happy Life* and *The Promise of Rest*.

fact of Mike's heterosexuality. Now I could work at learning whether there was a way to be some part (both useful and rewarding) of a threesome, a new adventure for me since my sense in early childhood of being a vital component in my parents' marriage.

Another day in Stockholm and a three-hour harbor trip by boat with Anne, Colin, François, and a friend of Vanja's named Berit. Then a full tour of Skansen—my calendar claims "monkeys, elephants, bears, bears, bears"—and dinner at the Black Sheep in the old town. Then Colin and I began our return to England the next day at noon. We spent a night in Copenhagen at the flat of an Anglo-Danish lady friend of Colin's (I slept alone on the sofa), then the long train trek again to Esbjerg where we re-embarked on the *Kronprinz Frederick*, shared a second-class cabin with a sixteen-year-old figure skater, and were on land at Harwich at one the next day. And I was in Merton by six with a mountain of gathered letters. I stopped to see Nevill for a few minutes, then dined alone at the Taj Mahal—the nearest Indian food in easy reach of college, before another long snooze.

In distant retrospect, the trip—and all the events of Mike's wedding—seems a likable one. I'd known from the time of our meeting in the fall of '55 that, whatever my own ongoing intense love for him, he and I would never spend our lives together. From within his own desire for women, Mike had given me an extraordinary amount of loyal care; and we've remained best friends, through his two marriages and my several romances, for fifty-odd years. Despite very different sorts of personalities and minds, it's remarkable how many assorted things we've meant for one another.

A quick leafing back through the calendar's numerous subsequent pages might suggest that my English friends—Nevill Coghill, David Cecil, Stephen Spender, John Craxton, Matyas, and a good many others—had nothing better to do in the rest of my second stint than entertain an otherwise idle American (which of course was not the case). There were frequent drives in the countryside for rural teas at charmed sites like Thame and Woodstock with dashes up to Stratford for Shakespeare onstage. There was a warm Christmas in Brighton at Anne's apartment with Mike and Vanja; numerous train trips to London for theatre, opera, gallery, and party visits with friends there. And Merton itself provided rewards. I knew very few undergraduates by then; but Oxford dons of that final halcyon year spent far more time with their academic colleagues—all male, as they still were—than they do today.

It's important to add that, despite popular jokes, very few of them were queer. I seriously doubt that the percentage of senior homosexuals in those days exceeded the percentage elsewhere in society (my guess is that the number of undergraduate queers was likewise in sync with the entire surrounding culture, and I'd found the same to be true of male students in the mid-1950s). A good many middle- and upper-middle-class Britons then had spent years in public schools—what Americans call prep schools—and queer behavior in those exclusively male cultures was inevitable, as it is in many other all-male societies. What was so different in my English years was the undiscussed commitment of a large number of adult men to largely male company. I'd never experienced such an arrangement among noncelibate men; and to this day I've never encountered another like it, certainly not in academic America, though some branches of the military offer likenesses. The loss of such a mature opportunity to know this male world is one more reason I greatly regret the gender mixture of present-day Oxford.

Some of the men, like David Cecil, had wives and children to whom they were devoted; yet the structure of college life, and ancient expectation, profoundly shaped their friendships (it was one of the sadnesses of Auden's disappointing return to Oxford in 1972 that he discovered how the old convivial life of dons dining and lounging with one another had largely disappeared). Though I knew several of the faculty wives fairly well, I suppose it's typically male-obtuse of me that I never asked how they felt about the social arrangements. The division of lives—wives as mothers and household managers, husbands as frequently absent teachers and scholars—obviously reflected the rigid division that preceded the profound alterations which came with the rise of radical feminism in Europe and the States in the late twentieth century.

For convenience's sake if I divide my year in half, from mid-July '61 till Christmas of the same year, I can see that the first five months went—with a few quiet exceptions—like a shot, though an often circling and looping shot. If I try, in retrospect, to explain why (though I'd been sure I could write in Oxford) I spent so much of my time racing round with my English friends, there seem to be two answers. The first is that, whatever I'd hoped, I proved unready to begin a second novel. In fact since the new fiction I contemplated was a complex family saga, at least another decade would pass before I had mulled its needs sufficiently and launched myself upon the work that became *The Surface of Earth* (and its two successors in the Mayfield trilogy). I was trying hard, at least thinking hard, writing copious notes, for a long story.

Second, the three years back in Durham had kept me busy with serious work in a far more disciplined way than I'd experienced in my first Oxford stint. And while I'd met enduring friends in those Durham years, I've mentioned that I had far too little of the conversation I'd learned to crave; and I'd had virtually no rewarding love life. In crucial ways then, Oxford was unfinished business for me; and I was hell-bent on finishing that social and sexual education. While I wouldn't return to D.Phil. work with David Cecil, I'd go on to learn a fair amount about the world I'd inhabit thereafter and about myself, much of it sad.

My relations with David and Nevill differed from our prior friendships in that—without their saying so—they now considered me a full-fledged adult, no longer a student; and they gauged our meetings accordingly. David had his family, so our meetings sometimes had an annoying unpredictability. He'd invite me to dinner, or say that he'd come to my rooms for tea and then phone the Lodge at the last moment to cancel. Once he even sent me an intercity telegram to postpone; a few times he simply failed to materialize (my Merton rooms had no telephone nor did any student rooms). In an amusing and illuminating memorial volume called *David Cecil: A Portrait by His Friends*, the novelist Anthony Powell describes a similar trait in David—

. . . apt to cut appointments, not over-good at returning books he had been lent. Indeed that was perhaps a somewhat frequent estimate.

I can't recall his ever co-opting a book of mine; but when he'd missed a meeting, he always promptly arranged a new occasion, which he generally observed. My best times with him in those months were his frequent and unannounced visits to my rooms in Merton—visits when we'd talk about a wide range of subjects. It was then that my sense, acquired years earlier from his public lectures, that he possessed a deep and unostentatious wisdom was confirmed. And this second time round, I asked him more than once for his advice on matters of personal love and other private matters.

Once when I'd just received a letter from my mother, who was disturbed at the prospect of my brother's engagement to a girl whose family were Roman Catholic, I brought the matter up with David who was a devout Anglican. At once he asked me about the girl's origins. I said that her family was Italian, only recently immigrated from Sorrento to North Carolina; and without further questions, David said "Ah, then I think you should tell your mother there's unlikely to be a problem." (His prophecy proved entirely true.) Then he paused. "If her family were Irish, I might be more concerned."

Whatever the nature of our talks, there was never an instance of condescension or unkindness, either to me or to any of the people whom we mentioned—unless we were speaking of political figures or literary critics who'd volunteered for fair comment. These times also he was far more relaxed in talking with me about his family and their home, grand as it was—how as a boy, he loved roaming through the vast archives of Hatfield House, the Cecil residence built by Robert Cecil in 1611 and containing nearby the old palace in which Elizabeth Tudor lived before assuming the throne. The secret letters from Mary, Queen of Scots, which had helped insure Mary's beheading by Elizabeth I, were great early favorites. More than once, when I was worried about something that seemed large, he'd remind me that his own mother had once said to her father-in-law, David's paternal grandfather, Robert Cecil—who as Lord Salisbury was Victoria's prime minister for many years—"Sir, don't you think it matters *very* much that I do thus and so?" And the old man (who'd, after all, managed the world's largest empire) said "My dear, nothing matters *very* much and few things matter *at all*." Then David might add "Of course it's worth knowing what those few things are." Since he was Christian, I thought I knew a good deal about David's list, though I never asked him to catalogue it for me; and he never volunteered.

But he never capitalized on the history or the ongoing influence of the Cecils (his elder brother Robert, for instance, was still a central figure in Conservative politics; but that was never discussed). And David never mentioned once to me that he and Rachel would each summer visit Elizabeth, the Queen Mother, in her country estate—she and David had been childhood playmates. And only once did he ever employ his title in my presence.

One morning I was with him in his study when he asked if I'd like to go with him and his son Jonathan to the New Theatre in Oxford that night. When I accepted gladly he said "But now I must find you a ticket." He dialed the box office at once; and when the ticket clerk said "I'm afraid that won't be possible tonight," David said quietly "It's Lord David Cecil here." As the clerk renewed her search for a ticket, David covered the mouthpiece of the phone, smiled to me, and said "The title is sometimes surprisingly effective in acquiring tickets." So it proved to be.

And though I had the old-time American fascination—especially a white Southern fascination—with British aristocracy (and though that played some part in my attraction to David from my earliest student days), such a magnetic draw played no significant part in my eventual sense of deep gratitude for his interest. Despite an occasional sound of faded Edwardian rhetoric in his written essays—a sound that drove his gruesome *bête noire*, F. R. Leavis, into near foaming seizures of rejection—I ultimately learned more critical truths from David Cecil than from any other of my teachers, ever; and by the end of that fourth year in Oxford, I'd come to a thoroughgoing love for him, a love that I'm proud to say appeared to be returned for the remaining years of his life.

Maybe I saw even more of Nevill. That was likely owing to the fact that, as Merton Professor of English Literature, he now lived in college; that he'd recently acquired a car and was eager to use it and that (as an unmarried man with no family ties—his only child, a grown daughter, lived elsewhere) he had more free time than David. As a man who'd decided years ago on his homosexual nature, he'd had no male partner and may never have had one; and surely such a relationship would have been all but impossible for a man who meant to go on living in college. In the course of the fourth year, Nevill introduced me to the man whom he called the great love of his life; but the man, then in early middle-age, was apparently happily married with children, had left Britain for somewhere like Malta (I believe), and had no thought of living elsewhere. So with all Nevill's numerous forms of delight—his teaching, friends, theatrical productions, and his frequent visits to the theatre—I often sensed a deep sadness in him, a never quite lifted air of loneliness—not usually intense but always present, despite the fact that I literally never heard him complain or speak of it.

Like David (though not so grandly), Nevill was the child of an aristocratic, artistically gifted, and quietly well-to-do family; and those origins gave him—like David—an inoffensive self-confidence that also permitted his love of good humor, in himself and others. He loved few things better than a laugh at some self-important fool's expense; and he generated a good many such jibes, entirely on his own and most often justified, though he also welcomed all other sorts of deflating jokes from others. The possibility of a meaningful unkindness, however, was unthinkable in his presence. In the years of our friendship—and it lasted, by mail at least, till he ceased corresponding shortly before his death—I never knew him to perpetrate a cruelty, however small.

In the first half of my second stint, there were the many dashes into the countryside for tea or dinner; and while Nevill was a considerably more attentive driver than the literally hair-raising David, he was not a world-class motorist. It's worth noting that at this point in British society, afternoon tea was still a very real intervention in the day's routine. Even at Merton several dozen young men would gather between four and five thirty in the Junior Common Room Bar for sandwiches, cakes, and some form of warm liquid—either tea or coffee—all before college dinner at seven. And on a few occasions in my English years, I had the almost anthropological pleasure of accepting a tea invitation from some elderly Briton (Edwardian era) who observed a ritual that was all but as steeped in social and emotional meaning as the ancient Japanese tea ceremony—fine china, cucumber sandwiches, a silver teapot, and an offhand set of serving gestures that were nonetheless predictable in their rhythm.

And however full Nevill's huge hands might be with an academic duty or, say, the proofs of one of his successful Penguin translations of Chaucer, it was almost unthinkable not to have at least an hour's pause for tea—an hour that was almost never observed alone. He could always of course walk across Fellows Quad and climb to the Senior Common Room where a few of his collegial Fellows would be available; but more often he'd invite some interesting visitor to Oxford or a recently discovered undergraduate actor to join him at 4:30. With Nevill, as with virtually every other human being in the English-speaking theatre, good looks were considered the beginnings, at least, of talent—he'd after all given Richard Burton his first major role.

More rarely his scout would serve a high tea with substantial sandwiches, a selection of excellent British cheeses, scones, butter, and marmalade—all laid on to fortify us for an evening at the theatre. Oxford itself could frequently provide, at the New Theatre, a new play bristling with famous actors on their way to the West End in London. At the university-owned Playhouse there was even more frequently some surprisingly good production by the OUDS, the Oxford University Dramatic Society. And of course Stratford-on-Avon was only an hour's drive north, with often excellent productions at the Shakespeare Memorial Theatre (though none to approach the Olivier-Leigh performances of *Macbeth, Twelfth Night, Titus Andronicus,* and the Gielgud *King Lear,* all of which

I'd seen at Stratford in 1955). Still, with Nevill I saw a good *Romeo and Juliet, King John,* and *Cymbeline.* We also saw a good, not great, *Richard III* with Christopher Plummer and Edith Evans.

I sent a letter to a friend with these notes: "The obvious, cheap thing to say about Plummer's *Richard III* is 'All very well, but he isn't Olivier'—which is true: he just isn't. But it's very brave to tackle the role with the memory of Olivier green in every head and though Plummer often passed up the perfect (i.e., the Olivier) way of a certain phrase or gesture simply because it was the Olivier way, he kept the whole thing moving tensely to the end. What I did learn from the performance (that I haven't from the highly edited films) is what a wonderful play *Richard* is and how—as always—silly scholars are who tossed it aside as an 'early work.' It's a tragedy, that's what, and in 30 years or so—when Olivier's memory has faded—maybe someone will suppress the comedy of Richard and play him as a tragic hero."

In his spacious college suite, Nevill was often host to meals of an unparalleled opulence in those days when English cooking had still not recovered from the deprivations of the Second War. Two meals are especially interesting memories. The first was a dinner held the evening of August 12 and involved old friends of Nevill's—all queer, I thought: Clifford Kitchin, a novelist; Christopher Scaife, the poet and composer; and L. P. Hartley who was not only a novelist of real distinction but also David Cecil's close friend. I was the youngest guest by thirty-odd years but, as always in my Oxford experience, was treated with the unspoken—and unearned—assumption of equality.

Of our table talk that day, I recall only one thing—or I think I do. Leslie Hartley had published his masterpiece, that finest book about a child, the near-perfect novel *The Go-Between* in 1953; and I'm all but sure he said that, when he was a boy in Dublin (he was born in 1895), he'd had pointed out to him on the street a very old lady who was Miss Brontë, the aunt of the famous Brontë sisters and their renegade brother, Branwell. Any such Miss Brontë would have been the sister of the novelists' father, the Reverend Patrick Brontë who was born in 1777 and lived till 1861—a considerable stretch then for Hartley's story; yet Patrick Brontë was one of ten children, and I still suppose the claim may be true. After all in 1966 I heard Alice Roosevelt Longworth, the daughter of Teddy Roosevelt, say that when her father was in the White House, she used to ride horseback with him out to Mount Vernon on a Sunday and that "the old gentleman who showed you round the place, his father had rowed Washington across the Delaware"—a claim which is also chronologically possible.

An even more extraordinary luncheon occurred in Nevill's rooms in November. The table seated some six of us—the poet Robert Graves and his wife, Beryl, David and Rachel Cecil, Nevill and me. Graves was the recently elected Professor of Poetry, Wystan Auden's successor, and had come to town for his first lecture. He was a tall man still, sixty-six years old. When he and I met, he recognized my accent and asked where precisely I was from. When I said "North Carolina," he said "Ah yes, my dear friend Ava Gardner is from Carolina." With his long history of extraordinary relations—even servitudes—to various women, I wondered just what the dazzling Ava would have to say about him, but I never had a chance to ask her. Over lunch he kept up a supreme egotist's steady monologue of interesting and occasionally appalling talk. He spoke of his early friend—and (I thought) great superior as a poet—Wilfred Owen and called him "that little homosexual"—two adjectives that were in fact accurate if dismissively spoken. And when someone happened to mention the dead critic Desmond MacCarthy, Graves likewise dismissed him as rude and inconsequential. Rachel Cecil, who was hardly given to combativeness, paused a moment and then said with her firm smile turned full on Graves, "Goodness, I never found that my father was either"—our poet hadn't known that she was Rachel MacCarthy by birth; but once informed, he gave no sign of caring. It was only then that his large head and face gave off the air of an epicene early Caesar, a man even worse than Claudius whom he'd portrayed so memorably in his novels *I, Claudius* and *Claudius the God*.

Just when most of us had heard enough meanness and self-aggrandizement from Robert Graves—and none of us doubted the strength of his verse, even in light of his absurd egomania—he learned from Nevill that Merton had recently converted a room in Mob Quad into a small museum for its old student Max Beerbohm. Nevill also informed him that David was at work on a biography of Beerbohm—upon which Graves at least partly redeemed himself with a memory and a poem.

He told us that he'd seen Beerbohm fairly recently near the old man's home on the Italian Riviera; that he seemed very much himself, very clear-minded. In response to a question from Graves about what work he might be doing, Beerbohm had said "Almost nothing." But then he'd remembered—"I *have* lately written one short poem," which he proceeded to recite. Then Graves recited it to us, a memorable limerick. At the end of the luncheon, I raced back to my room and wrote it down. In the ensuing forty-five years, I've seen no mention of the poem; so the following version—as true as I can make it—is what I recall.

> *There was a young lady from Hythe*
> *Who said, "I am lithe, I am blithe,"*
> *But then Father Time*
> *For the sake of the rhyme*
> *Just mowed her right down with his scythe.*

Soon after that, Nevill's party rose; and we all walked with the Graveses a hundred yards to the Beerbohm room and then to the college chapel to see the lovely statue of the Virgin. Later in the year I heard more than one of Graves's disappointing, and sometimes loony, professorial lectures but never met him again—and would never have tried to. An incidental illustration of the fullness of the year is indicated by the following diary-record of the remainder of that short day.

After the Graveses' departure, Nevill and I drove into the country, to Long Wittenham Clumps; then back for tea and a dash to the Playhouse to hear Kenneth Clark lecture, but there were no seats. Feeling understandably a little sick, I napped for two hours; then by eight I rallied and went to a small party in Julian Mitchell's rooms on Canterbury Road—a party that offered the relaxed company of other writers, all of them far more likable than Graves—Dom Moraes, John Fuller, John Bayley, and of course Julian himself. Well after midnight I walked back to Merton and climbed in over the low Grove wall—the gate being locked in those days at eleven (and I, though a member of the SCR, had failed to ask for a key).

The third friend whom I saw often was, again, Stephen Spender. Though he continued to live with his second wife, Natasha, and their two children on Loudoun Road in London, the family had been offered the use of a roomy and very pleasant redbrick cottage (a middle-sized house really) adjacent to Michael Astor's estate near Burford and the village of Bruern. Stephen was still coeditor of *Encounter* and continued to spend a fair amount of time at his duties there. He was also writing steadily on several large projects—his long autobiographical poem (unpublished even now, though likely his most important work), a commissioned translation of Schiller's German play *Mary Stuart*, and his usual burden of articles and reviews. He likewise continued to traverse the planet restlessly—partly for the necessary money to support his family, their considerable establishment in London, his art collection, and partly from his lifelong restless hunt for people and places of genuine interest to him (he had a lifelong dread of boredom, perhaps a dangerous trait in a writer). By the early Sixties then, though Stephen was only in his early fifties and still possessed of much curiosity and eagerness, I could see that he was wearier at heart than he'd been when I first knew him.

He spoke with me at length, and wrote to me, about the unhappiness in his marriage. The relation he'd begun with a young man named Osamu in Japan in 1957 had sputtered out in a bitter aftertaste and the realization that a whole large need of his sexual nature had not been satisfactorily met for many years, and he was even less content than he'd been in the job at *Encounter* (later in his life he said to me that he'd been "truer" to his homosexuality than to anything else in all the years).

He was remorselessly harangued by many on the English left on the grounds that he was surely working for a journal financed by the CIA (what was the origin of their certainty?). His repeated efforts to get a straight answer from the Congress for Cultural Freedom, the reputed backer of the magazine, had met with continual runarounds. Yet though he could get no straight answer from his employers, he was not prepared to quit. The position was distinguished; and it paid him decently without requiring a daily nine-to-five commitment, though its demands for his attendance at frequent international meetings and endless-talk conferences were plainly exhausting and eventually humiliating.

He and I never discussed the matter at length; but in retrospect it seemed almost too simple an explanation to say that, since his recent poetry had met with bad reviews and he'd withdrawn from publishing more of it, the eminence he commanded as editor of

Encounter gave him more continued satisfaction than anything else available in the early postwar years. Further, his commitment to an ongoing married life and the expense of raising two likable and intelligent children required a respectable salary (in addition to the small income he had from inherited funds; incidentally I never asked what he made at *Encounter,* and he never mentioned the sum). More than once he told me that he could leave "all this" tomorrow and live a life of far greater simplicity; yet several times he told me how he worried that my simpler life would imperil the richness and depth of my own work.

And he knew that both of us well understood that he could never leave the complexity of his choices; as it were, it proved they'd have to leave him. Before his impulsive first marriage, he'd lived (with his eventual partner Tony Hyndman) his own simpler life—unluxurious travel and the company of friends as remarkable as Isherwood and Auden. For whatever reasons—the pressure of social respectability perhaps, his sleepless intellectual and artistic curiosity to be sure— he'd soon made the decisions that had tied him in the Gordian knots of his own perhaps insufficiently foresightful nature.

For all that, though, he remained a mostly cheerful, always generous-hearted and encouraging friend; and we spent a good many times together—some in the racket of London and New York but even more in the deep country quiet of the cottage in Bruern or my quarters in rural North Carolina where Stephen would work for hours in his own room and I in mine or outside in the sunlit greenery. Then we'd meet for quick lunches or longer dinners, mostly cooked by Stephen (who was a plain but skillful cook).

Early in the summer of '61, he invited me to London for lunch at the Café Royale with Christopher Isherwood who was in England for one of his rare visits from California. As long as I'd known Auden and Stephen, I'd never met Isherwood who was their closest companion for a good part of the time the two younger men had spent in prewar Germany and elsewhere. In fact it was Isherwood who'd accompanied Auden on a trip to assaulted China in the late Thirties. On their return to England, the two men passed through the States and soon made their decision to emigrate there in '39 before the Second War began (though Hitler's announced intentions were ominous). Eventually Isherwood had anchored himself on the West Coast while Auden remained in the East with the eventual love of his life, Chester Kallman. Auden supported his life by writing and teaching, Isherwood immersed himself in screenwriting and—unexpectedly—in a sect of Hindu philosophy called Vedanta.

I had admired Isherwood's fiction for years—his famous Berlin stories (famously about the narrator's homosexuality without ever quite saying so) and his early novels and memoir—so I was all the more interested in the chance of a meeting. At once I could see how little he'd altered in appearance from the very short, wiry, and beamish young man who appears in early photographs (the beamishness had diminished a little, though the quiet charm had not). And right away—a little to my surprise—I took to him. Like his old friends he talked freely and amusingly; and whenever he and Stephen laughed over some shared memory, Isherwood would turn to me and explain the point of their amusement. When we parted in Regent Street after lunch, I hoped to see him again and know him better; but I'd encounter him only once more, in '64 when I was in Los Angeles at work on a screenplay. There I encountered Isherwood with Don Bachardy, the artist and much younger but longtime companion who'd be with him many more years, till his death in fact.

I was taken to our second meeting by the director with whom I was working (Jack Garfein), and our hostess was the actress Natalie Wood. It was a small Christmas afternoon party—fewer than twenty guests—and Wood herself was warm and welcoming (she was between her two marriages to Robert Wagner), but my memory is that Isherwood and Bachardy stood apart from the others and seemed to decline the high spirits, though with no trace of scorn. The fact that Isherwood was then on the verge of becoming one of the most visible defenders of homosexual rights, far more so than Auden or Spender, may have had something to do with his chosen separateness that day. Whatever, I managed to tell him of my strong admiration for his recent novel, *A Single Man*—still his masterpiece and the eventual subject of a responsive film. Four decades later his fiction is still little known in the States, though it much repays reading for its unnervingly clear-eyed, sharply focused gaze.

Soon after the lunch in August, I drove out to Bruern with Stephen and Lizzie who by then was an increasingly beautiful nine-year-old, still passionately interested in horses. It was a bright weekend, and John Craxton soon joined us with a strikingly handsome friend named Jim from Malmsbury. Then midway through the weekend, John Bayley and Iris Murdoch came for dinner. It was likely my first meeting with the two of them since we'd joined for tea at Redmayne's in Burford on my first stint. But I'd met John early and often in my friendship with David Cecil and had liked him at once. He'd been David's protégé, had written one good army novel early on, then moved into teaching at New College and writing first-rate literary criticism—lucid yet deep and mostly directed at the great nineteenth-century Russians. He was a charmingly small, balding, and slightly bent man whose intense stutter could be a problem when it came to attending to his voluble and often humorous conversation; but since it didn't faze John himself, I always soon overcame my unease in his company.

Though Iris was well on in her second career as a novelist (she'd begun as a philosopher), she was generally quieter than John. But she appeared to have forgiven me an earlier carping review in *Encounter* of a novel of hers. She smiled very fetchingly; and though she was a few years older than John, she had a studiously boyish look under her Botticellian cap of Irish hair. When she spoke her remarks were mostly pointed, well worth hearing and often witty; and without at all claiming that she behaved seductively toward me, I was not surprised to read in biographies after her death of the very active sexual life she'd led before her marriage—in her reserve she was nonetheless almost disturbingly attractive. As usual, Stephen cooked the evening's meal, with fumbling help from all the rest of us round him in the kitchen; and the night went swimmingly. My calendar says that John and Iris stayed till near midnight (Johnny Craxton and Jim stayed for another night).

I don't recall seeing John and Iris again that year, though—in response to an invitation from me—she did come to a party Harry Ford gave for me in New York in the early 1970s (she was there for a lecture at the American Academy of Arts and Letters). John Bayley's later published accounts of her slow disappearance into Alzheimer's disease in the 1990s are almost unbearably sad; yet for all the undemonstrative heroism of his loyal care through the worst of her illness, almost till her death, her ending seemed no great amazement. She'd always seemed a creature on the verge of *leaving*, having quietly left behind her a tall stack of good books—departing the room, one's company, the world, the planet, and this unsatisfactory universe at least. On that happy evening at Bruern in August '61, not even the fiercest prophet could have foreseen on our laughing summer night together the mixed fate of Iris and John—her mind's departure and John's ongoing devotion. Nor could I—then as strong as a lean-limbed young ox—have foreseen the calamity that struck my own lower body twenty-two years later but has left my mind, such as it's always been, intact in its usual housing (so far, so far).

In fact, it would be honest to note here that in such gatherings as I've mentioned in the past few pages, I was still a cipher in the eyes of all the grandees I met, not to mention those I'd encountered in prior English years. Such a generous host as David or Nevill or Stephen might introduce me as the writer of a forthcoming novel, might even mention stories of mine which had recently appeared. In an excess of his famous generosity, Nevill would call my Rosacoke "the best woman in fiction since Jane Austen"; but there were months to go before *A Long and Happy Life* appeared in the shops. And I had considerable private awareness that, for now, I was a man on the verge of thirty who could offer these lavishly gifted tables no more than a dense shock of black hair and a willing laugh. (Iris and John had at least been sent a bound galley of the novel, but had yet to mention it; maybe the memory of my condescending *Encounter* review of a novel of Iris's hadn't faded after all. And maybe I should add, for clarity's sake and as unobtrusively as possible here in a parenthesis, that sexual favors had not been requested of me by anyone; nor had I given the slightest sign of being on that not uncommon brand of make.)

Before I move on from Stephen's early contributions to my stay, I should note that soon after my arrival, he'd asked me to write a story for the forthcoming hundredth number of *Encounter*—a special issue with a cover by Henry Moore and contributions from Auden, Forster, Orwell, Stephen, and a cast of thousands. I was to represent the Young. I'd first suggested something like "A Child's Christmas in North Carolina," a narrative that would be very much my own but might nonetheless parallel Dylan Thomas's celebrated "Child's Christmas in Wales" (and Price is a common Welsh name). Stephen had approved my idea on the spot; but as I began to rethink the prospect, and to reread the Thomas story—richer than any Yuletide pudding—I knew the idea was a poor one for me. I very quickly thought of a story (I figured it had to be a story; I couldn't just describe Christmas-as-a-boy after Dylan Thomas's thing), but of course as I commenced to write, I saw how complicated the whole thing could be—and probably ought to be—so soon I was in a very Hamletish dilemma. Shall I dash off three thousand words for the hundredth number—just so I could keep company with all those Stars—or should I take my usual year or so and torture out something more complicated? Stephen was vague, but I gathered my deadline would be the first week in October. The obvious answer was, well sit down and write three thousand words and if it's good send it in, and if it's not—burn it, eat it, bury it. I then suggested to Stephen that I write a story concerned with the old man—Grant Terry—who'd been intimately involved with my family since before my birth and had, more than a few times, actually lived in our house.

I'd only recently become aware that Grant might have been born a slave (he apparently didn't know his birth date, but the possibility then seemed real that he'd been born before 1865, the date of actual emancipation); and I'd always been curious about the powerful bond that he and my father had formed long ago. My idea suited Stephen and I went to work on it. Again the hope of a long story, even a novel, which I'd brought with me in July had proved recalcitrant; so the new idea was more than welcome. And when Stephen proposed that the highly original and prolific Australian painter Sidney Nolan might be willing to illustrate my memories of Grant Terry, I was all the more impelled (a lunch meeting with Stephen and Nolan in London in October promised Nolan's cooperation; I took at once to his antipodean warmth and wit).

The other Spender event from those early months doesn't con-

cern me directly; but Stephen phoned me on November 17 to tell
me, with much laughter, the following remarkable story. I didn't set
it down in writing at once; but Stephen kept me informed of further
developments as they occurred in succeeding days, so here at least
is my memory. A day or so before his phone call, Stephen had been
invited to a small luncheon with Evelyn Waugh (I think the hostess
was Mrs. Ian Fleming). Waugh had always extracted as much satiric
fun as possible from the Auden, Spender, Isherwood group. In fact,
in his novel *Put Out More Flags* he'd introduced two characters—
Parsnip and Pimpernell—who were clearly based on Auden and
Isherwood. And as decades passed, Waugh's own Col. Blimpish
conservatism, domestic stinginess, and repeated mean-spiritedness
had become a perpetual source of bemused news reports from his
assorted venues. Nonetheless of course in 1961, masochistic Stephen accepted the luncheon invitation with some hope of repair-
ing old animosities.

And lo, the occasion seemed to go well enough. Then toward
the end of the meal, Waugh pulled out his antique gold watch and
said "Damn! It's stopped, I'm in a frightful rush for my train, and I
shan't have time to take it to my jeweler in Regent Street" (or was
it Bond Street?).

Stephen readily flung himself into the breach, said that he'd be
going right past the shop on his way back to the office and could easily leave the watch off. To Stephen's amazement Waugh accepted
the offer and handed over the handsome eighteenth-century heir-
loom.

Whereupon Stephen put it in his own pocket and—of course—
forgot to stop at the jeweler's. When he realized his omission, the
shop had already closed; and he thought it was no great matter. He
could take it in the following morning. Meanwhile he returned to
Loudoun Road and put the watch in a drawer in his study.

That evening he and Natasha gave a small dinner party—my calendar says "for the Beatniks" (I'm not sure which ones). Among the guests was Francis Bacon, the painter, who as ever arrived with one of his gangster boyfriends. The evening proceeded with relative calm; and on the guests' late departure, Natasha went downstairs to clear up in the kitchen. In no time she called back up—"Stephen, the spoons are missing!" (their antique silver spoons). In another instant Stephen's heart nearly seized. He strode to his study, opened the concealing drawer—and Evelyn Waugh's watch was gone. What could have been worse? He'd welcomed a gangster into his home—the lover of a world-famed notoriously drunken homosexual painter of wretched men wrestling on sordid beds (or so Waugh would surely define the matter)—and now Stephen's conciliatory gesture lay in irreparable ruins.

It was a sleepless night on Loudoun Road, and at near dawn he managed to contact Francis Bacon. Stephen said "Francis, your young friend may keep the spoons; but the watch must be returned." He explained the history of his request. When Francis defended his friend from the charge, Stephen only repeated the offer—"He may keep the spoons; the watch must come back."

More anxious hours passed. Then late in the afternoon a taxi pulled up at the Spenders' door; the driver got out and rang the bell. When Stephen answered, the man handed over a crudely wrapped parcel—"A gentleman has asked me to deliver this here." Thank God, it was Evelyn Waugh's gold watch, unharmed for all its recent adventure. The entire situation would have made—almost *should* have made—an episode in an early Waugh novel. And of course it could only have happened to Stephen who'd only lately come to be called a Holy Fool in articles—a man like those perhaps mildly demented figures in old Russian novels who traveled the roads as quasi-saintly figures, throwing themselves on the mercy of others.

I stress again that I tell the story from memory, though it's one I've heard Stephen tell many times through the years since his half-confessional, half-hilarious phone call to me in the Lodge at Merton (the only place I could receive calls). If I've made a substantial error in this latest telling, then at least no living human is likely to be harmed by my version—all the principals are dead. I myself never met Waugh; still, I've admired some of his work, especially *Brideshead Revisited*. But it may be worth recalling at the end of this episode that—before Stephen's loss of the watch—I happened to mention to David Cecil that I'd recently seen Henry Lamb's large portrait of Waugh as a young man who looked especially chilling; and David said "Well, yes, he's a very bad piece of work indeed."

As the year spun toward its close, Matyas and Sofia were married at the Oxford Registry. A boyhood friend of Matyas's named Karol, who'd shared his Nazi incarceration and now lived in London, came to town; and he and I served as official witnesses to the brief and charmless ceremony. The weather was unusually warm as Karol and I walked with the newlyweds back through sunny streets toward Merton for a wedding luncheon. As we proceeded along Ship Street, laughing as we went, Karol suddenly burst into even higher laughter. He'd just noted that, from an overhanging tree branch, a small bird had shat copiously on my shoulder. Of course I said to myself something like *That truly puts the tin lid on it!* But once Matyas and Karol had recovered from a gale of laughter, they assured me that being shat on by a bird was, in their native country, considered great good luck. Since it was the second wedding I'd attended since summer—each marriage involving someone whom I loved—I needed perhaps more bird shit in my life.

The fact truly was, however, that by winter I'd recovered from any serious disappointment I'd felt when Matyas had informed me of his hopes in his new relation with this young woman. In the ensuing five months, I'd seen a good deal of the two of them together and grown to feel real affection for Sofia. Not only was she lovely to see, she was as affectionate as she looked; and she'd never given the least sign of rejecting me because of the little she knew about my prior relations with Matyas (she herself had endured, fairly recently, the painful end of a long romance).

What, though, was I doing with my own always considerable head of sexual steam? It's easy enough, at this point, to be both truthful and brief—*nothing* (nothing that wasn't self-powered). Doubtless there were outdoor venues where willing gents met in the dark, and there may well have been further pub venues up Cowley Road in the vicinity of the Morris Motor Works where the clientele might well have been of the sort that excited Oscar Wilde some eighty years ear-lier (he described his own adventures with the working class as *feast-ing with panthers*). I don't claim an excess of virtue in my avoidance of such possibilities. One of the prime chances had worked for weeks just downstairs from my room in Mob Quad.

There was a young man involved in the large job of cleaning the blackened and scarred stone walls of the quad through the whole summer of my second stint. Almost all the colleges were then involved in such cleaning and replacing of the many stones which had suffered, in the past few decades, from the chemically ruinous effects of combined car exhaust, coal-burning furnaces, and rain. The young man was remarkably handsome—maybe twenty-three and very Italianate in his looks and his warm response to a show of interest from someone else (Roman soldiers had after all occu-pied Britain for some three centuries, and their DNA had no doubt intermingled widely with the natives). He was always eager to talk whenever I'd stop and detain him from his spraying and scrubbing. He was quick to tell me that he'd recently come out of prison where he'd been detained for "'ittin' a bloke wiv a bottle." Since he'd spent

The artist John Craxton, on the left, with a friend, likely Jim Moss. This was shot in late-1950s London.

twenty-six months in Lewes Prison, it must have been quite a bottle. He told me about his girlfriend and his motorcycle. I'm sure if I'd asked for a ride, he'd have cheerfully met me after his workday ended; and God knows where we'd have ended up—he had that deep glint of readiness in his dark eyes. After he finished his work at Merton and departed, I spoke about him to an interviewer for a London magazine that was covering the publication of my novel. When the story was published, I began to worry that he'd see it and be offended (I didn't give his name but the other details of our acquaintance appeared in the article).

Then one day soon after the magazine appeared, I saw him coming toward me on the High. I was tempted to duck into a shop, but he'd seen me and waved. When I stopped to speak, he laughed and said "I saw that piece you wrote about me." I said "I hope it didn't bother you"; and he said "Oh no, I quite liked it—I don't get a lot of publicity, you know." Then he laughed in lieu of elbowing my ribs. I was fascinated that his phrasing at least implied that he truly thought the interview was dedicated to discussing him when perhaps he was only choosing the barest minimum of words. In any case, it was a charming encounter; but I think that was the last time I saw him.

Why? Very largely I think, because of one of my few reasons for shyness. I dread rejection. I was also, maybe rightly, reluctant to grow well acquainted with a man just recently freed from prison and with—I soon learned from one of his workmates who was still at Merton—a pregnant girlfriend. Yet a number of my bolder friends—Johnny Craxton, for one—would have arranged on the spot to meet him in a pub and explore the possibilities of a further acquaintance. But in the stone cleaner's case, and all others I might have pursued in those early months, I genuinely feared entanglement—or was it commitment (and do they generally differ?). So the usual abstinence of my prior three years at home continued.

If I partly thought I was conserving my energies for work, I was deluded. Early on, as I said, I'd given up on the idea I brought with me from home. What did happen, though very slowly, was further attempts at perfecting my old short stories and the new work on "Uncle Grant." In between those jobs, and all the social activity, was a good deal of final housekeeping on *A Long and Happy Life*. Harry Ford at Atheneum seemed content to send me more and more sets of proofs so long as I wanted them. And I was often interrupted, in whatever English chore, by interviews arranged through Chatto, Atheneum, or *Encounter*.

Even now I can summon, with only a few seconds' thought, the excitement of that crescendo as it built toward publication in the spring of '62. And I cut a deep trench, walking up Merton Street on past the Bear Pub, and the north-side wall of Christ Church to reach the vast and busy main Oxford post office in St. Giles and mail back to London or New York some hefty packet of proofs or interview response or the photographs I'd had made by Edmark on the High for requested publicity purposes back home.

Had I simply emptied my writing chest when I finished the novel? Likely I had and—proud of it as I was by the drumbeat of progress toward publication—I was slowly digesting my first big dose of writer's uncertainty: would I ever have another verbal impulse as potent as the one that fueled *A Long and Happy Life*; if so, would I know how to set it down forever? Though by the end of '61, I'd finished "Uncle Grant" and revised my early stories till they all but squeaked with polish, it would be the late summer of '62 (and back at home in the States) before I returned to work on a sizable piece of fiction which confirmed—to myself—that I was in fact a writer, not a one-shot burnout (that story would be a long autobiographical piece called "The Names and Faces of Heroes," the completion of my second full-length volume).

Or was I somehow paying for my solitude, the welcome state that fueled so much of my childhood and all my earlier work? The last few pages above clearly indicate that I was hardly alone, almost any day at Oxford. But I was now a full-grown man (in age anyhow); and I had no wife or male companion, no welcome partner beside me in bed. I don't recall dwelling on the fact in those fallow months of '61. Yet if I'd truly wanted such company, or thought I needed it, why had I not made far more serious efforts to find it? I hadn't failed to see that my main attractions might just be for men whose own desires were preset for women.

Was I unhappy? Nothing that's endured in memory says I was. In the midst of such attentive friends, I had almost no time to think of sadness, though at Merton I was in the unaccustomed position of living in the midst of more than a hundred undergraduates but knowing virtually none of them—I was, to them, essentially a Fellow that year. Why did I make no serious efforts to know students (a single exception is discussed below)? Even the English weather of those years—dark, damp, and chilly as it still was before the recent benign effects of global warming—failed to oppress me as it had before—this time, I suppose I knew what to expect and braced myself for it. Yet whatever my surviving memories of the time, it may be worth noting that my calendar has three widely spaced remarks which speak to the question.

I mentioned that I'd spent the afternoon and evening of August 7 at work on a complete revision of "A Chain of Love" (the first draft of which I'd written seven years ago). No basic structural changes but hundreds of minor operations on the language to remove the last of what Bill Styron called "Dixie Baby Talk" (the sort of Southern talk which is absolutely accurate but on which Eudora Welty has virtual squatters' rights), and I thought the story much stronger. At least I could read it now and not hear whole stretches of it in

Eudora's voice. At bedtime I noted in the diary "Alone and working, I am happy." I'd had a pleasant afternoon walk with Roger Highfield, the Merton history don who was nearly twenty years older than I but who'd preceded me in what seemed to be a contented single life. That was the beginning of a week that spelled hope that whatever else might happen, during this year I would become the writer I wanted to be.

After Monday's revision of "A Chain of Love" on Tuesday I did more or less the same job on "The Anniversary" which I really liked now, though I never did before. Most of it was first written in that same room in 1955 so there was justice in redoing it here, after six years. In the morning I had a letter from Doubleday saying that "The Warrior Princess Ozimba" was being considered for the next O. Henry volume. (It had appeared in the summer *Virginia Quarterly Review.*) Also on Tuesday I had lunch and spent the afternoon with my old American friend Mary Johnstone who was newly thin and more than ever like a grave Botticelli boy. She was in the process of moving to London where she would teach in the fall, so she was in and out of Oxford often.

Mary came back on Friday afternoon. I had been sick the previous night and all morning with some mysterious nausea, but she cheered me enough to make me suggest dinner to her. When I returned, I found my transistor radio (Bill's actually) and my electric razor stolen. The police came and "investigated"—i.e., asked a lot of solemn questions. The only thing that worried me about it was not the sixty-dollar loss (that was covered by insurance) but the fact that all clues pointed to an Inside Job, which would mean either my scout or one of the neighboring scouts, and if proof were found then it would be up to me to swear out a warrant—or not. In any case he'd lose his job. One funny thing was that the thief didn't take my two cameras (mine and William Blackburn's) or my traveler's checks or my typewriter—just the two small, easily concealed things. I'd never been robbed before so there was an element of the exciting Unknown about it—for instance, I kept waking up all night wondering if he'd return to the scene, but he didn't. On the heels of that loss and insult Saturday morning ended the week with a fine and unexpected surprise. The mail brought another letter from Doubleday with a check for $108—royalties on my share of the last O. Henry volume. It was a total surprise and, as I'd overspent in Sweden, a very welcome one.

On September 8 I wrote ". . . feeling lower than I have yet this summer, thinking: I must work this coming week or consider returning home." By the end of the second week of December, after staying a night with Matyas and Sofia in London I found myself alone and lonely in a deserted and ghostly quiet Merton. And on December 15, I came toward the end of the year with this note—"A day in which I spoke to no one except shop-attendants. Eichmann sentenced to hang" (Adolf Eichmann, the Nazi official, then on trial in Israel).

Two days later Mary Johnstone came to visit (after a month's silence) and renewed her invitation to visit in Leeds, but I detected a considerable coolness in the offer (she had just got engaged). My friend Andrew Hook had invited me to visit him in Edinburgh, but I wrote my regrets, explaining, "With conscience clamoring, I reckon I must decide against Edinburgh. The real reason is that I've just begun the story which should finish—at last—the volume, and I'd be courting literary disaster to halt now for however pleasant a reason."

However grim those entries sound—and I was nearing the end of the year's shortest day—I'd soon have a warm Christmas (Mike and Vanja Jordan were on leave from his job in Washington and were visiting his mother on the south coast in Brighton). I took a train the day after Matyas's wedding, arrived late on December 23, and spent three full days and nights in Anne Jordan's apartment—old and young friends and family relations stopping in regularly with great lashings of good food; and a long walk with Mike and Vanja on the almost deserted seafront and the shingle beach, memorable photographs of which survive, no cause whatever for regret—though my return train to Oxford was delayed by a frozen switch at some crucial junction in the tracks. The trip which should have taken two hours wound up taking four, and all the train carriages were heatless for some reason—another of the unexplained joys of nationalized railroads.

Once back in late afternoon on the twenty-sixth, I found the Merton gate locked; but in hopes of not having to climb in somehow with my suitcase, I knocked loudly; and Arthur Major, the perfect lodge porter—another old bachelor—opened for me with his Cheshire-cat smile. In my rooms in Fellows Quad (by then I'd moved there, staircase 1, third floor) my breath made clouds in the cold air; and it took hours, with my small electric heater, to bring my space to a life-restoring warmth. At least the power was on; so I bundled up, made tea, and sat reading *War and Peace*—for the first time—in hopes of tiring myself out enough for bed.

Then at 7:15 in a virtually empty college—cold dark all round me—I heard steps begin on the ground floor and slowly rise the three stories of wooden steps to my door. It was a little too much like a childhood ghost story for comfort—*The ghost is on the first step; now it's on the second*. Then there was a solemn pause and a knock. I'd heard more than one quite sane senior man tell stories of inexplicable apparitions in the Oxford quads. (Nevill had one of his own, involving an old lady who knocked on his door at Exeter College under similarly unlikely circumstances. As he opened on her, the lights in his room suddenly went out. He begged her pardon but by the time he managed to find a working lamp, she was of course gone.) So I may have actually blessed myself—I should have at least—and said "Come in."

Wally Kaufman—a Duke student of mine who'd become a good friend and was now in his first year at Merton as a Marshall Fellow, doing a B.Litt. in English—was back from his December month in Spain. He'd taught himself fluent Spanish through the years by keeping a journal in the language; and while he'd traveled on a student budget, I was surprised to see that he'd lost ten pounds and grown a full beard. He was wearing a long poncho, heavy boots, and gloves; and if he'd tried to look more like a Renaissance gentleman returning from Christmas at his father's country manor, he couldn't have succeeded more thoroughly.

Lonely in the holiday aftermath, I was glad to see him—a student of mine, after all, to prove my life as a fake Merton Fellow was not entirely fake. We'd hardly glimpsed one another before we knew we were famished as wolves. So we climbed out of the locked-up college to find some supper. All the midtown restaurants were shut—bolted and dark. We walked on up the Cornmarket then, counting on the usually trusty Welsh Pony, a familiar pub near Gloucester Green. It was open and we gorged ourselves on hearty saloon food—pork pie, roast potatoes, and Christmas cake. Once filled we climbed back into Merton and talked ourselves into flat exhaustion, Wally collapsing for the night on my sitting room floor since his own rooms were locked and he'd misplaced the key.

In the New Year Wally would be the closest of my younger friends; and while his various girlfriends consumed a number of his evenings, I continued to feel a strong draw toward his many differences from me. I was hardly from an upper-class family so far as wealth was concerned; and in those days Wally had likely overemphasized his working-class background, but his Long Island

Stephen Spender and Wallace Kaufman at Bruern. Wally had recently arrived
for study at Oxford on a Marshall Scholarship. Reynolds captured this image
of two friends in clear pleasure.

accent and the rich personal mythology he'd woven round himself—his father's early death, his mother's mental agonies and suicide attempts that resulted in several hospitalizations, his childhood rivalries with older twin brothers—made us different enough to give us a good deal to talk and argue about. In fact, we were quite capable of differing from one another with a near-violence of intellect, a difference so intense as to leave us speechless in one another's presence for several days to come.

Yet during those months at Merton, through a good many small-scale ventures together—jaunts to London, movies in Oxford, the sharing of friends—we developed a mutual respect and affection that served us for decades more of friendship when Wally returned to live nearby in central Carolina through more than one marriage, the rearing of a daughter, and an eventual seismic shift from left-wing politics to a stonier conservatism, many long trips to various states of the old Soviet Union, and an eventual decamping to life in the Oregon woods (whence I hear from him sporadically).

Stephen was away from England for a good deal of early '62, so my main contact in London was John Craxton. On into late winter I maintained the possibility of going to Greece—to Xania in Crete—where John was considering the purchase of an old house (he even raised the question of my going in with him on the purchase, though Stephen privately warned me against owning what he called "absentee real estate"). On John's advice I even went to the Oxford Health Department for my second smallpox vaccination and a series of typhoid shots. As spring neared, though, two things weighed against the prospect of any significant time in Greece. The first was John's characteristic uncertainty in the face of any firm decision on his own travel plans, second were the pleasant rumors that A *Long and Happy Life* (scheduled for publication in the States and in Britain in March) was likely to get an unusual degree of critical attention as well as financial success. Shouldn't I be back at home to enjoy that long-sought phenomenon?

So by late winter I'd decided to head for New York and North Carolina in late spring. Meanwhile I spent a good many days and nights in the unique Craxton home on Kidderpore Avenue in Hampstead, a household that the pianist Denis Matthews called the center of London Bohemia. A tall late-Victorian house, it sheltered a number of assorted Craxtons in those days; and I came to know them all as well as our different ages permitted. John's father, Harold, was the son of a pub owner yet became one of the premier piano teachers in Europe (a teacher who had a longing to compose). He received his pupils in an enormous ground-floor studio at home, and John's mother, Essie, ran the teeming establishment with an apparent (though slightly brow-furrowed) ease that surely belied heavy loads of concern — making her laugh was a serious chore, yet her kindness was impeccable.

No doubt unconsciously Harold Craxton generated a distinct Mr. Magoo–like comedy of benign oblivion to the busyness all round him. John's witty and warm sister, Janet, was one of the chief oboists of the BBC Symphony and could generally be heard practicing upstairs — near John's own large studio and in the rooms she shared with her partner Alan Richardson, one of Harold's students. And in the early spring of '62, John's older brother Antony, a stellar producer of BBC Television (especially of programs about the royal family), moved temporarily back into his parents' house to explore new trajectories in his own private life — that is to say, his suddenly declared queerness after years of marriage and family.

Antony was often in residence during my visits, and I found him always amusing and helpful in considerably more reliable ways than his highly gifted but often vague brother John, who seemed mildly annoyed by Antony's fresh revelation. All the younger family residents became enduring friends; and to enrich the mixture, there were almost always houseguests (like me) or day visitors ranging from men and women of high artistic eminence to an Iranian student who helped with the cleaning and cooking and provided a welcome statement of silent dignity, just with his own strong face and ready smile — much remindful of a princely countenance in an antique Persian miniature painting.

And now that I speak of pictures — in the five years I'd known him, John had always said that he meant to draw or paint me. On one of my visits, he finished a red chalk drawing of me near a window reading (it began when he and Matyas and I visited the Scilly Islands and was completed later in London). I begged at the time to purchase it. But in his maddening way, John refused to sell the picture; and it was only some thirty-five years later that Matyas wrote me that he'd stumbled on the drawing in a presently ongoing show of John's portraits in London. I phoned the gallery at once and, in under five minutes, finally acquired the picture — along with an ink and wash drawing of Matyas.

Those middle years of his career had not been a bountifully productive time for John. His focus on Greek subjects for his paintings — shepherds, dancing sailors, sun-baked landscapes — seemed at least temporarily exhausted, though his portrait drawings (Greek and otherwise) had absorbed the better part of his considerable store of a visual tenderness that was nonetheless unsentimental in its linear clarity. My own portrait is a strong reminder of that gift; for me it's another live relic of my own happy days and nights in the openhearted, and entirely original, Craxton household. I've only just learned that 14 Kidderpore Avenue is now managed as a rehearsal studio by one of Harold and Essie's grandchildren — at least it's in the family still.

Reynolds Rhia.   ·Craxton·55·

A sketch of Reynolds drawn by John Craxton when Reynolds was staying at the Craxton family home in London. Reynolds tried to buy the drawing at the time, but John refused. He was able to purchase it many years later from a British dealer.

If there was a surprise in the year, it built gradually toward the spring. I've said that, increasingly in my three first years in Oxford, David Cecil took a more than routine interest in my work and ultimately in our friendship. After the three-year hiatus in Durham, that friendship continued to grow. Since I no longer had a car, I reached meetings with David either by walking to his rooms in the Front Quad at New College or I took a city bus to his family home on Linton Road or he came to my rooms in Merton. As always he wasn't especially good in keeping appointments; what was new and pleasant was David's tendency to sudden unannounced visits to where I sat reading or ceaselessly revising my old stories. I'd hear footsteps up to the third floor; and when I opened the door, David would say "Send me *straight* away if you're more gainfully employed."

Invariably I welcomed him; but it's only now, almost five decades later, that I see how he'd come to be for me something I very much still needed, close as I was to my thirtieth birthday—that is, a father (David was born only two years after Will Price, thirty-one years before I was born). Not that he ever assumed paternal airs or took familial liberties. I've said that he had his own much-loved family; but he added me, with increasing frequency, to the small list of friends with whom he met often in Oxford for the kinds of conversation in which he was brilliant, though hardly self-preening or overriding (few of his brief spoken paragraphs ended without a question—"Do you agree?"—or "Perhaps you feel otherwise. Tell me.").

As the year progressed, and we met more often, my calendar noted on April 15 that "we talk much less of literature now." And I go on to list some of our unplanned informal subjects—marriage, children, friendship, homosexuality (several of his close friends were queer), religion, magnanimity. If I were compelled to choose a single word now to describe David Cecil, I couldn't choose one that was truer than *magnanimous*; and I'd do so in full awareness that *magnanimous* and its noun *magnanimity* contain two Latin roots connoting *great* and *soul*. After this fourth year, we'd meet twice more in the States and once for an especially warm visit with him and Rachel, after his retirement from Oxford, at their rural home in Wiltshire; and we corresponded often. Apart from my father and mother, I miss no one more than David Cecil.

If I saw a little less of Nevill Coghill in the winter, it was likely owing to his increased involvement in teaching and in work on his Penguin translation of Chaucer's *Troilus*. During the winter term I attended his course of Milton lectures. By then I'd spent a good deal of my study life on Milton's poems and found myself often demurring from Nevill's unmitigatedly enthusiastic treatment, even of the earliest poems—though given the ongoing powerful influence of T. S. Eliot's and the dreaded Cambridge critic F. R. Leavis's rejection of Milton, an outright enthusiast at Oxford may well have been part of Nevill's strategy. In any case Nevill shared my own sense that, in English, only Shakespeare had displayed gifts equal to Milton's and that on more than a few occasions Milton exhibited understandings and verbal skills that had escaped even Shakespeare; so I never conveyed my disagreements to Nevill. He was too eloquent a standard bearer to risk discouraging—and after all his years of teaching, he was still surprisingly open to discouragement.

Matyas was newly involved in his marriage, though Sofia continued her job in London, coming to Oxford mainly on weekends. I went to dine with them in Matyas's rooms on Valentine's Day evening (an unconscious irony, I assumed). They told me that they were expecting a first child in October—old-fashioned quick work for a couple married just before Christmas. They'd retained Sofia's pleasant flat in London, and they welcomed me to stay with them on a few weekends and during their Easter trip to the continent.

I continued valuable friendships with other old friends—Tony Nuttall and his wife, Mary (having completed his classics degree, Tony was embroiled in graduate study in English and would become one of the most original of literary critics, especially of Shakespeare; but first he gave me great help in reading the steadily arriving proofs of my novel).

I occasionally saw my old Headington landlords, Jack and Win Kirkby, as well as Jim Griffin with whom I'd paid a long Christmas visit to Italy near the start of my first stint (Jim was the only member of my class of Rhodesters to spend the remainder of his life in England, as a philosophy don at Keble). In my three-year absence, Win had taken driving lessons and bought a small car. One evening she called at Merton and invited me to drive out with her and a female friend to dinner in a nearby village. I gladly accepted and a great deal of laughter followed (as well as a few white-knuckled terrors in the backseat of Win's car—I've mentioned the scary driving of Nevill and David, and Stephen and Wystan Auden—but Win took the prize: the challenge of concentrating on the road before her was more than her love of talk could agree to).

Stephen's son, Matthew Spender, paid me several visits. At seventeen now, he was beginning to look seriously at possible Oxford colleges for his own imminent university days; and his mother delivered him to Merton more than once (eventually Matthew would become a much-admired painter and sculptor as well as a biographer of his deceased father-in-law, the painter Arshile Gorky; and we've remained in good touch).

Julian Mitchell was on a fellowship then at St. Catherine's College; so we had numerous chances to affirm the friendship we'd established when he'd stayed with me in my Durham trailer (before long he'd begin a successful career as a novelist, a playwright, and a screen and television writer). Julian drove me out to his family's home in the Cotswolds once, and we made several trips to London in his car. There were two other joint experiences that proved indelible.

In mid-April we went to Covent Garden for a performance of *Tristan und Isolde* with Birgit Nilsson and Wolfgang Windgassen. I note in my calendar that Nilsson's Isolde, strong as it was, was "safe but always underneath for me was Flagstad like a palimpsest" (I'd heard Flagstad's Isolde during her penultimate season at the Met in '51). That Covent Garden evening with Nilsson was the notorious performance in which, during the entire first act, she wore a long cape that had only recently been dyed a corrosive shade of green. The dye had not had time to dry; and as the long act proceeded, Isolde's hands and arms grew inexplicably and unnervingly a morbid shade of green—a color that couldn't entirely be removed for the remaining two acts.

Next morning Julian and I went to the National Gallery to see Leonardo da Vinci's near life-sized drawing for a proposed painting of the Virgin and Child with St. Anne, the Virgin's mother. It had just been purchased for the nation from a private collection in England; and despite the fact that the drawing bore little resemblance to Leonardo's unfinished painting of the same figures, it was still as beautiful a picture as I'd ever seen (and it remains so)—a sepia drawing, larger than any I'd previously encountered. A week later I went back to spend more time in its astonishing presence. The thought that a human being had caused it, and with one human hand (a left hand at that—Leonardo being left-handed). Though I've seen it only once again, I admire it, in memory, as much as I did in its presence. There may have been more likable painters than the sometimes chilly Leonardo, but no other has—for me—reached such heights of otherwise unimaginable sublimity.

And remembering the company of friends in those months, it had been good too to see Mike and Vanja several more times since Christmas and to give them, as a wedding gift, a large handsome Craxton ink drawing of a street scene which John was barely persuaded to sell me. Mike was then at work with an international agency in Washington, but he traveled a lot and Vanja accompanied him on some of his European visits. Mike was very much his old self—extraordinarily even-tempered and attentive to his friendships. The inevitable change in our relation had proceeded gradually enough to preserve the best of what we'd shared—long talks, much amusement, silent but unquestioned loyalty on both our parts. And Vanja and I established that rarest of marital pleasures. In short we built a friendship that, though it hardly excluded Mike, grew and deepened on its own—especially as she bore their three children, all great favorites of mine (and the elder boy, Nick, my godson). The ability, acquired after hours of practice in my own early childhood, to reproduce the voice of Walt Disney's Donald Duck with apparent perfection was my passport into their lifelong friendship—and that of numerous other children of friends. Vanja and I have even continued to think warmly of one another, though at long distances, after the end of her marriage to Mike (even so, it lasted more than twenty years, far longer than many).

Steadily occupied with so many friends, again it's hardly surprising that I managed little new work. I craved the pause. And then my attention was increasingly jangled by the various excitements attending the publication of a first book, one on which I'd worked to the exclusion of so much else. First there'd been the proofs. Then there'd been a gathering beat of indications that the book was bound for success—the acceptance by *Harper's* of the entire novel for publication in a single issue, the November celebratory dinner at the Garrick Club hosted by my editors at Chatto, Peter Calvocoressi and his colleague Cecil Day-Lewis (the poet and father of a five-year-old boy who'd become the actor Daniel Day-Lewis), a series of contracts for translated foreign editions, and the praiseful sentences from various older writers.

The better publishers declined, in those politer days, to call them *blurbs*—an ugly coinage by Gelett Burgess, an early American humorist; still, I was mildly astonished to learn that certain Oxonians deplored my acceptance of praise that they looked upon as suspicious. The oddest behavior came from a young critic who, at our first meeting at a very small drinks party of Matyas's, literally assailed me verbally for the encomiums of critics and writers whom he looked upon as very old hat.

As publication neared in Britain and the States, I was interviewed sympathetically by three widely read periodicals—*The Saturday Review* in the States, *About Town* and *The Manchester Guardian* in England. I was also interviewed along with Raymond Williams and Frank Kermode, on the BBC's *Bookstand* at the Lime Grove Television Studios in London. Fred Coe, the American director, offered a film option of $50,000. I agonized over the wisdom of accepting such an offer, with its surrender of aesthetic control over my story and characters. David Cecil told me that I "mustn't scorn $50,000"; and ultimately I didn't, though the film was never made. Paperback rights sold to Avon in the States for $35,000 and to Penguin in Britain for something less. Those sums would amount to roughly six times more today, and they were coming to a young man who'd scraped pennies through all his adult years.

Then in late winter at last I received bound copies from Atheneum and Chatto. Having the finished book in hand—a literally palpable object—was a fulfillment of hopes that extended as far back as my early adolescence (and farther, if I consider that my love of painting from age five or six was a prematurely focused longing for a life in the arts). But by age sixteen I'd begun to see—largely through a growing awareness of world art—that in that world I couldn't be more than an excellent copyist. Having scented a flair for verbal expression (that I began to show in the eighth grade), two splendid teachers nudged me firmly toward writing. So since I was no good at the prime boyhood virtue—sports—I trucked right onward. Was my own experience, by the age of sixteen and seventeen, so complex that it needed written expression? And given my parental families with their engrained gifts for narrative speech—which almost always resulted in plain storytelling—didn't my hopes for writing constitute an irresistible expression of an entire family's need and delight? And the family involved is not merely my own genetic circle, but the whole history of humankind—our undiscourageable story-generating species. I said in my preface to *A Palpable God*

A need to tell and hear stories is essential to the species *Homo sapiens*—second in necessity apparently after nourishment and before love and shelter. Millions survive without love or home, almost none in silence; the opposite of silence leads quickly to narrative, and the sound of story is the dominant sound of our lives, from the small accounts of our days' events to the vast incommunicable constructs of psychopaths.

If the answer to either of those earlier questions is *Yes, my early experience was complex enough to require written expression* and *Yes, I was also maintaining a vital tradition of both my parental families,* a minor third question might be this: if the complexity of your experience had left you with an overpowering need to deliver yourself of written stories, then why did you—a queer man—produce stories, long and short, about more conventional men and women—the kind who married and produced both you and your brother as their immediate offspring?

Since I've spent the remainder of my writing life in deep narrative concern with just such people—though there are at least queers-in-the-making in my stories from as early as "Troubled Sleep" which I wrote in '58—I can affirm that it's been my general desire to write about the kinds of people who comprise the huge majority of the human race, the kinds of people who've likewise been the majority of my kin, friends, and loved ones. And does it need saying that the greatest homosexual writers have done the same—the poems of Michelangelo and Auden; the novels of Melville and Proust, Virginia Woolf and E. M. Forster, not to mention the plays of Tennessee Williams among a good many others?

In the early spring of '62, when the reviews of *A Long and Happy Life* began appearing in Britain and the States, I had the elation of receiving largely superb reactions to my story. Soon the praise was mounting as a kind of custard atop an unnerving smaller dollop of critical dislike, even a very rare occasional notice that seemed to originate—though out of the pen of a perfect stranger—from some sort of personal hatred. It's a reaction that's as bizarre to me now as then. Considering the very small number of novels that can be said to have harmed real portions of the human race (and I can think of none, though Goethe's *The Sorrows of Young Werther* is sometimes claimed to have set off a wave of suicides among young German students), how can a given novel elicit the sorts of verbal mayhem that one sees regularly in the reviews by such otherwise mild-mannered organs as *The New York Times Book Review* and now the often savage voices of the Internet? Stephen Spender who—God knows—had received dozens of such reactions (as well as perpetrating them in reviews of his own) said to me, a few years later, something that I've repeated to myself many times as a soul-saving mantra—"If you do your honest work, there will be people who hate you for exactly the same reasons as other people love you; and you will never resolve this paradox."

As the vest-pocket clamor of reception continued, in late March I took a crack train—the Scotsman—from London north to Edinburgh to visit a young Scot with whom I'd taught at Duke. Andrew Hook had done several years of graduate study at Princeton before coming to Duke, and now he'd returned to Edinburgh to begin his work as a teacher and critical writer. Wally Kaufman had gone north separately at the same time, to visit an old girlfriend who was studying there; and when we all joined up for several good evenings, I felt considerable relief from the mild bruises of my ongoing reviewers' pillow fight (pillows with an occasional flat iron concealed among the feathers); and incidentally I've never in my life replied to a negative review.

Returning to Oxford I began the always melancholy chore of packing (even the job of stuffing an overnight bag depresses me). With my promised new capital, I'd booked return passage for mid-May in a private cabin from Southampton to New York on the recently launched French liner, the *France*; and with Matyas and Sofia's offer of their apartment in London—and the offer of two or three sofas in Oxford—I departed my rooms in Merton and began a month of gypsy life commuting between the two cities, both of which were now such troves of glad memory that I've seldom revisited them—so as, presumably, to leave the happy memories intact.

With only three weeks before I'd embark, I met at the Craxtons' a young man whom my calendar first describes accurately if laconically as "a 19 year old American dancer." I'll call him Ben Holman. He had the classic male dancer's body—medium height and lean as a well-turned walnut table—with packs of muscle in calves, arms, shoulders, and back. His family was part Jewish and his face was appropriately endowed—winning large eyes, black hair, a strong jaw. His demeanor was mostly grave but with welcome outbursts of laughter. He was from New England and had recently gone to New York to study dance with Martha Graham. While there he'd met an English choreographer of very considerable promise in London, a man named Norman Morrice who'd later become director of the Royal Ballet and die, unmarried, in 2008.

That older man had been visiting New York for a look round the local dance scene, especially Martha Graham's company; and when he and Ben met—to hear Ben tell it—the attraction was mutual. An intense affair ensued, troubled as it was by the Briton's fear of exposure. Even good dancers could apparently be terrified in those days, though the homosexuality of male dancers was all but a universal joke—wasn't it Oscar Levant, the pianist, who called ballet "fairies' baseball"? After a short while, Morrice returned to London, telling Ben that any thought of continuing their relation was out of the question. Convinced of his own love at least, Ben soon followed Morrice to London. As soon as Ben phoned to announce his arrival, Morrice reacted sharply. He'd meant what he said; his English career could be ruined by further contact.

Still undeterred, Ben took a next step. If he could only find work in the sizable London dance world, he could fund himself for whatever time it took to think through the tangle and engineer a way toward a feasible relation with his spooked friend. Meanwhile Ben had met Tony Craxton—John's brother—and Tony was acting as a kindly temporary shepherd for the rather stunned boy. There was no sign of an intimate bond between the two; and on the evening of my own first meeting with Ben, John and Tony Craxton went with Ben and me "to Pinocchio for very nice funny dinner"—Pinocchio was a likable Italian restaurant which I'd discovered weeks earlier in Soho.

The next day after John, Wally, and I had seen Buñuel's hair-raising *Viridiana* at the Curzon Cinema (London's chief venue for foreign films, further distinguished by its location on a street then famed for strolling whores and the still-standing home of Georg Friedrich Handel), we returned to Kidderpore Avenue. There was a message awaiting me—Ben had phoned from his Bayswater Hotel and asked if I "could come round sometime for tea." A little oddly John advised me against further contact with Ben, then returned me to Matyas and Sofia's flat. I failed to reach Ben that night but rang him at nine next morning and asked him to Oxford for the day (I had some last chores there). He accepted at once, I collected him at eleven, and we raced to catch the 11:15 from Paddington.

Going straight to Merton, we checked in with Wally; then went to a local restaurant for lunch (a favored though frequently disappointing but now-and-then tasty place, famously characterized by its waiters' startlingly dirty fingernails). Over lunch for the first time in our acquaintance, Ben began to talk at length about something called Subud and to ask if I was aware of the work of Gurdjieff and Ouspensky (I wasn't at that point). He also said a good deal about his *atman*, another new word for me. Later, Wally would say that Ben was a pure Isherwood character—a quick but keen observation. In my calendar I agreed that he was; but I also added "there is enough humor and irony—and charm, and also more than a hint of depth and goodness."

Whatever, we spent more of the afternoon than I'd intended trying to contact the Oxford chapter of Subud (or Ben did). Finally success; their meeting was at eight. Then as Ben and I were walking up the Woodstock Road in full sun, David and Rachel Cecil passed in their car, saw us, pulled over, and invited us to Linton Road for a later drink. After tea with Wally, I rang for a room at the King's Arms Hotel in midtown. We checked in there and went to the Cecils from six till half past seven—talking mostly of ballet (which everyone but me was well informed about). Among the pleasures of that visit was the chance to introduce David and Rachel to a friend for whom I felt a growing attachment, however recent.

I read alone in Wally's room till Ben returned just past nine. After initially telling me about Subud, he seldom had much more to say about it; and I never asked, though I saw its urgent importance for him. And eventually I learned that it was an organization devoted to the spiritual growth of its members through the practice of certain exercises that are believed likely to assist in that development. For all I knew, it was Ben's main prop through this romantic shipwreck he seemed to be enduring in the face of a flat refusal from the man who'd accepted his attentions in New York, however briefly. (Again, I'm recording Ben's version of the story, never having met Norman Morrice.)

We had a late supper, once more at the gloomy Café de Paris. Ben was a vegetarian and we'd already had one meal at the vegetarian restaurant to which Stephen had introduced me years earlier. Before ordering any meal, Ben would consult the menu slowly and thoughtfully, in search of a dish that his body felt it needed, then and there. (Did I suspect that something absurd was at work in more than one instance here? Yes, but then Ben was nineteen, an early age among American middle-class men.)

Afterward we walked on in the dry spring evening through three long blocks to our minuscule room at the King's Arms. Just beyond the twentieth-century cross-street Bridge of Sighs at Hertford College, the hotel nestled against Wadham College, of which the infamous Sir Maurice Bowra was Warden. (Not for nothing, one heard, was Wadham fondly called Sodom at Oxford—this Bowra was the Warden of Sodom and a classical scholar whose essays are monuments of dullness.) The long night that followed may, at least temporarily, have helped Ben repair some part of his sadness by assuring him of skills he possessed; for me at least it's a memorable night still.

*   *   *

We returned to London the next day and went together to Covent Garden to see the Royal Ballet in Frederick Ashton's *La Fille mal gardée* from 1960, a long narrative marked chiefly by attenuated youthful charm. Afterward we returned to Matyas and Sofia's where we had the flat entirely to ourselves and could assemble a cold late supper. Ben was cheerful enough; so not wanting to rain on any significant pleasure he might have taken in the evening, I asked how he'd felt about *La Fille* and was relieved to hear that—like me—he was disappointed in all but the attractiveness of the young men and women. Primarily he was only marginally entertained by Ashton's faux antique (modern dance being Ben's great love). Once he'd expressed his feeling, I was free to tell him that unspectacular dancing, in whatever genre, was no main love of my own nor was any other form of less-than-splendid performance art. I can still summon dazzling memories of Margot Fonteyn in *Cinderella* on the same stage in '56, but then *La Fille* did not plan to be spectacular.

I spent the next weekend with Mike Jordan's mother in Brighton, then back to Oxford for Julian Mitchell's birthday and a night on Matyas's sofa before returning to London about noon where Ben and I watched the interview I'd recorded earlier for the BBC's *Bookstand*. It was my first experience seeing myself on television; and it gave me the uncanny sense of watching my brother (at that point we looked so much alike). Having Ben nearby was an outright help in adjusting to the shock; alone, I'd have been jarred to the point of sleeplessness. As it was, we slept too late.

Next morning I was in a serious rush; and Ben went with me to the Cromwell Road air terminal, a choice that surprised and pleased me. I left Heathrow for a peaceful flight on Alitalia to Rome, arriving in midafternoon and heading for the Pensione Bellavista Milton by bus and taxi. For years Stephen and I had talked of meeting in Rome at some point and sharing a few of its splendors. He was off now on one of his far-distant journeys, but we'd made plans to join up in Italy at last. With my several new slabs of income, I might have thought of a more ambitious hotel; but I chose the one that had rescued me and Jim Griffin from our cheerful whores on Christmas seven years ago. The same desk clerk greeted me with grave recognition, from behind his classic enormous nose, and sent me on upstairs to a rather garish double room. There'd been an unfortunate redecoration since my last visit.

I took the nap I badly needed, then walked a few blocks to the Veneto which was quiet in the light of late afternoon; then back and down the always welcoming Spanish Steps lined with azaleas in enormous pots (the window behind which John Keats died in 1821 was just overhead). From there I crossed over toward the noisy Corso, past the Caffè Greco (deciding to wait till Stephen was here for tea in those small rooms so dense with memories of the long-gone great—Byron, Goethe, Berlioz, Wagner for instance). Then feeling how tired and a little sad I was by then—sad for young Ben in London and me in Rome, suspended between this city and home, and each of us a quart low on love—I circled back to the Milton and had my dinner alone, with a little reading in Edmund Blunden's calmly horrific memoir of trench warfare in the First War, then to sleep by ten.

I woke early, breakfasted in bed—a soft-boiled egg, two rolls, the usual apricot jam, and coffee—and slept again till ten. It was pouring rain at the window, so I spent the remainder of the morning reading indoors. Stephen arrived in early afternoon, seeming none the worse for his own long flight; and we lunched at the Milton. Soon we were laughing almost as ever, I felt remarkably restored; and by then the rain had relented. So we launched ourselves out, walked a long distance to an ominously deserted P.O. to collect an inevitable cable for Stephen; wandered through the deserted Forum and upward to the Palatine Hill for an hour (through the remains of thousands of caesars and senators), then had coffee off the Corso and—eventually—dinner nearby at a small but first-rate restaurant Jim Griffin and I had discovered on my first days in Rome in '55— Piccolo Mondo on the Via Aurora.

My diary notes that it "was unchanged in its indigenous prices and quality but filled with mid-Westerners. Alain Delon put in a momentary but gleaming appearance." Perhaps the Americans, me included, drove him off (though no one but me seemed to recognize him). After seeing *Rocco and His Brothers* a few days before I had sailed for England, I regretted not having Delon seated nearby for an inconspicuous study. Just the three minutes he spent in exchange with the manager left me with a certainty I've had no occasion to deny—he was the finest-looking young man I've seen, before or since, and a first-rate actor when challenged. Like Vivien Leigh in England, his early career was marked by the snarls of reviewers who curiously—instead of feeling lucky that their own ambitions as commentators had coincided with the career of so gifted and beau- tiful an actor—clearly felt that his personal beauty somehow deval- ued his acting. Several distinguished directors strongly disagreed with them—Visconti, Antonioni, René Clément, Joseph Losey, and Volker Schlöndorff; and a glance at the long list of Delon's films suggests that, in the spring of '62, he may have been in Rome at work on another Visconti masterpiece, *The Leopard* with Burt Lan- caster and Claudia Cardinale.

Next morning we taxied to the Vatican Museum only to find the Sistine Chapel inexplicably closed—the eternal mystery of Italian museums. Still, we spent the rest of the morning roaming the miles of generally mediocre sculpture, a few great paintings, and vitrines filled with astonishing manuscripts—the immaculate italic script of Michelangelo's poems, Botticelli's line drawings for the *Divine Comedy*, and various crucial papal bulls. After lunch and a nap, we went out to purchase tickets for the opera next day; then we walked back to the Vatican and spent the remainder of the afternoon there, roaming St. Peter's beauties and awfulness. I finally gathered my courage and kissed the all but kissed-away foot on the famous statue of St. Peter himself—the spot from which a woman in an Isak Dinesen story contracts syphilis (from a prior infected kisser who has just kissed the same spot).

More naps—the usual tourist exhaustion—then a taxi to Piazza Navona for a bracing dinner at the small but excellent Tre Scalini, a textbook example of the restaurant run by various members of one family (grandmother, father, mother, male and female children, all unobtrusively warm). Then—the first surprise—after dinner we were circling the dark piazza when Stephen suddenly said "My God!" Just ahead, half turned away, stood Stephen's old friend the English essayist Cyril Connolly and his young wife, Deirdre, dabbling at the fountain. I hadn't seen Cyril in more than three years, and I'd never met his new wife. Stephen said "Let's just walk up silently," and we did (who but Stephen could come to Rome and collide with a famous friend?).

At the sound of Stephen's voice Cyril stepped back slightly as though accosted. Then he inspected us carefully and, with his characteristic satyrlike half smile, gave us each a kiss on the cheek and said "To what do we owe this honor?" We explained our presence; then we all climbed into a tiny taxi and went to Doney's on the Veneto for brandy till eleven. Cyril, though famed in Britain for his critical ferocity and urgent prose, had always been extraordinarily kind to me; and the teasing kindness resumed the moment our first sips of brandy went down. We soon learned that the Connollys were staying at the Hotel d'Inghilterra and would be in the city for several more days with no major plans. We could spend relaxed time together then.

Another surprise next morning—on a staircase at the Milton we came across the English actress Gwen Watford. Stephen had recently worked with her on a play of his own, and it turned out that she was in Rome to play the unfortunate wife of Julius Caesar in the notorious *Cleopatra*, a colossal film epic that was at the moment in the process of rapidly bankrupting Twentieth Century–Fox. We'd known that the project was under way outside the city at Cinecittà—every newspaper reader worldwide knew that much—but we'd had no thought of encountering anyone involved. So we paused with Watford on the stairs, Stephen introduced us, and she explained her presence here—they all had the day off.

As we parted Stephen said "When you next see Richard Burton, please give him my regards" (he'd met Burton years ago).

Watford smiled and left. No more.

We spent a good part of that day repeating favorite sites of my own and Stephen's—Michelangelo's *Moses* in the church of San Pietro in Vincoli (Moses still looked alarmingly like Charlton Heston who was soon to play Michelangelo in *The Agony and the Ecstasy* in 1965); then Nero's spooky and largely subterranean Domus Aurea, followed by a good long sunlit sit-down in the Colosseum, and a return to the Milton for lunch and a rest. Then we walked to the opera for a 5:00 p.m. performance of *La Bohème*. The calendar confirms my memories of a "coarse performance but lovely moving music." And as many times as I've listened to recordings of *La Bohème*, I've still never seen it again onstage. Terminal public weeper that I am—real floods of tears—perhaps I've avoided it for that reason: I'd exit with swollen eyes and red-spotted cheeks. Rodolfo's final cries of "Mimi!" for his just-dead love are almost intolerably real and wrenching.

We walked back in a calm warm evening and met Cyril again at Doney's. Deirdre was not with him; and Cyril eventually explained that she'd stayed at the hotel, thinking we wanted an all-male evening. Stephen took care of that at once. We three boarded a taxi, sped to the Inghilterra, and persuaded the tearful Deirdre to join us for another excellent dinner at Tre Scalini, then all back to Doney's again for brandy till past midnight. "Good day," the calendar says with likable economy.

It records three more days with much the same pleasures — steady sunlight which, in almost that little time, wiped my slate clean of the winter rains and indoor chill in Oxford and London. We managed at last to see the Sistine Chapel (which we'd each seen more than once before). However much candle soot and other contaminants might have drifted upward since Michelangelo completed the job in 1512 (a four-year effort) — and before the drastic and questionable cleaning of the 1980s — the calendar says that the chapel was "packed but almost more beautiful than ever."

Next morning before we left the Milton, there was a phone call for Stephen from Richard Burton's secretary. Could we join Mr. Burton tomorrow for lunch? The answer was obviously Yes, and a certain amount of excitement ensued — even among the Milton's staff (it turned out that Burton's secretary had identified himself to the pensione's operator; and the news traveled widely throughout the building, with no help from us — understandably enough). Not only did *Cleopatra* seem bound to bleed its studio to death, it had apparently also destroyed Burton's and Elizabeth Taylor's marriages. The two preeminently world-class stars of that decade had very recently bade farewell to their mates and were reputed to be locked in mutual embrace, in private as on the screen (incidentally, there are no film or television stars today who can equal the media and screen fame of those two). Would we lunch with Miss Taylor also then? Since she was hardly a year older than I and had always been one of my favorite stars, I obviously hoped we would.

To cool my premature pleasure, I accompanied Stephen that day to a small luncheon quickly mustered by the British Council when they learned that Stephen was in the city. At a smallish table I was seated by an imposing and pleasantly talkative Italian woman who bore the name of Donna Alicia Borghese: otherwise I'm sorry to say that the occasion reinforced Stephen's frequent lament on the subject of cultural bureaucracy and staggering dullness. Yet he'd spent more than fifteen years — since the end of the Second War — in attendance at so many such meetings and pointless debates. Now and then he might encounter a new eminent acquaintance whose conversation, or more often wit, had redeemed some long journey. But by the early Sixties, he was seeing far more clearly — and discussing with me — what a dreadful amount of time and energy he'd lost in such well-meaning pursuits. And he could have so easily declined the British Council's invitation to take up half our day in Rome yet he hadn't.

Why? After long reflection, I can suggest only two reasons — first, at bottom he had some belief in the long-term value (especially in the heights of the Cold War) of such international merging of ideas and creative results. Second, at a time when his own poetry stood at an all-time low in critical repute, these alternate chances at another kind of creative eminence may have been irresistible. Better to be an internationally famed literary figure, perhaps, than an aging and cuffed-about boy-genius poet. And it's simply true to observe that he was the only British literary figure of high world standing in his time (Graham Greene might have surpassed him, but Greene's fetish of utter "honesty" and outspoken anti-Americanism made him always a kind of admired but dangerous Catholic and left-wing intellectual outlaw).

I've never regretted the warnings I registered in watching my friend's after all willing entrapment in such a blood-letting grip. His puzzling later fascination with the French and British wealthy came largely after his shame (when *Encounter's* ties to the CIA were revealed); and it may have been a partly comprehensible surrender to pleasure—good food and wine, access to fine houses and yachts and international gossip, and a reward he could offer his wife when the marriage had so many weak patches.

Despite the fact that John Sutherland's meticulous biography gave Stephen's enemies (especially those in the tiny frog pond of British literary comment) a chance to trot out their familiar—and occasionally justified—accusations of his foolishness, none of what I say above should deny or dilute the fact that during our days in Rome—and almost always through nearly forty years of friendship— my quiet conversations with Stephen revealed him as the most profoundly intelligent (and witty) reader I've known. I've praised a few others here highly as well, but no one else ever went quite as deep as Stephen in his discussions of poetry, fiction, and drama (which is not to say that I always agreed with him). And no one else was as keen an observer of our mutual colleagues in the business of writing. Any one of his encouragements, or his warnings, concerning my connections with another writer was always worth careful attention.

However dull lunch might have been, that night's dinner was maybe the best of my year. We joined the Connollys for a drink at the Inghilterra which lived up to its name, the England, with heavy dark Victorian velvet drapes in the lobby and massive carved mahogany chairs—perhaps an odd choice of hostelry for one as inclined to continental culture as Cyril. Then we all went out for dinner at the Casina Valadier in the Borghese Gardens on the very edge of the Pincian rock. Stephen and I had discovered it earlier on a walk through the spacious park (the same wooded roads were avenues for whores after dark). The word *casina* in Italian does not imply a gambling establishment, only a small house. There was nothing especially small, though, about this house designed by Giuseppe Valadier in the early nineteenth century; and the evening's weather was warm enough for us to dine on a roofed-in porch that opened onto the gardens.

The restaurant had distinctions above and beyond its good food and the kind of Italian service that, in those days, was well above anything I'd encountered outside Rome. In an essay called "How I Wrote Augie March's Story," Saul Bellow recalls that he'd worked on his novel at the Casina every morning for six weeks, smoking cigars and drinking coffee, and that the waiter informed him of the poet D'Annunzio's earlier love of the place. Bellow also mentions that Goethe wrote one of his tragedies nearby in the gardens. Very recently it also had been the scene of a first assignation between Vivien Leigh and Warren Beatty in Tennessee Williams's sad story of bought love, *The Roman Spring of Mrs. Stone* (not only was the story sad, the film was the next to last of Leigh's screen performances, made shortly after her divorce from Olivier).

As the youngest member of our own party, I noted in my calendar that the evening was "wonderfully funny," though I recorded none of the details of my laughing last meeting with Cyril (I do, though, recall that when Stephen mentioned our forthcoming luncheon with Burton, Cyril's smile deepened; and he said something like "Well, of *course*, my dear"—implying some amusement that his old friend and fellow founder of *Horizon* had come to Rome in hopes of an entirely quiet few days yet suddenly was bound for lunch with someone who was—at the moment—surely the most world-famed man residing in Italy, much less Rome).

After breakfast next morning Burton's secretary phoned with

another question. Would we care to have lunch with Mr. Burton *and* Miss Elizabeth Taylor? The combined entertainment press of the planet would have killed for the opportunity; and we were being asked if we'd object to such a joint event. Stephen said that we'd be pleased, and the secretary said that a car would call for us at the Milton at noon. Stephen and I went out for a walk in the brilliant sun (passing the great tenor Giuseppe di Stefano, who gave us a smiling bow in passing) and returned a half hour before a large black American car arrived to get us, a car chauffeured by a sleekly Americanized Italian named Mario. And from that point, in my calendar, I kept the most detailed notes of the year.

Mario drove us out, past the Colosseum and the Arch of Constantine, and some eight miles farther on the Via Appia Antica (the old Appian Way); then turned left onto a reasonably modern, lavish-looking house. Before we were fully out of the car, Burton was descending his steps to meet us, in polished cotton trousers and a white polo shirt. He seemed a little tense and "a little *loose* around the jaw," I noted.

We entered a large tall living room, and at once Burton said "I'm sorry my wife is in London." In the past two days I'd read enough in celebrity magazines to know that Sybil—the only woman Burton had actually married—had left Rome a few days earlier with their children, presumably in the face of a blizzard of speculation on the relations of Burton and Taylor. He then introduced us to what the calendar called "two tiny American boys . . . who seemed quietly queer." It turned out that they were visiting friends of Burton's secretary and "had been allowed to meet Stephen."

Thereupon a large tray of Bloody Marys appeared and the drinking began. In only another few minutes, Richard (which I'll call him hereafter; he invited me to at once) said "Miss Taylor is so sorry to miss seeing you, but it is stipulated in her contract that she can suspend work when she has her feminine period" (there'd be more about that stipulation as the day progressed). For now I concealed my disappointment, and Burton proceeded with a carefully honed skill that warmed the conversation quickly—he began to tell actor's jokes. I noted "all the Ernest Thesiger stories" (none of which I'd heard)—especially those centered round Thesiger's love of genuine pearls and the fact that he always wore a long strand of them, concealed on his person under layers of clothing. Burton then moved on to uncannily accurate imitations of the voice and movements of Peggy Ashcroft. Most amusing of all was his reproduction of her stage performance of Shakespeare's Cleopatra—"She looked as though she was just going out to fry up some chips." And that brought him round to the *Cleopatra* film.

His revealed willingness to joke about himself, as well as older colleagues, emboldened me to exercise my own curiosity about the film and its reputation as a huge disaster. I asked if it was going to be a good film. Richard took a long sip of his drink. "No, but it may be quite interesting" (I entered the day's notes on my calendar before bed that night, so I feel confident in quoting the principals). Next I vaulted onward to a question that, I could see, unnerved Stephen. "Is Elizabeth Taylor good?"

Richard's reply was startlingly candid. "As a stage actor, naturally I'd say 'Not really.' But she does some very extraordinary things. And she *is* so marvelous-looking, though she tends to sudden jowliness and to washerwoman's arms. But she has these *violet* eyes you could dive into." Imagine saying that to a stranger whom he'd met less than half an hour before; couldn't I have returned to the Milton, phoned some major celebrity news outlet, and sold my revelations for a sizable sum—*washerwoman's arms*? In recompense for the candor, he continued that he—and their co-star Rex Harrison who was playing Julius Caesar—could not manipulate the camera with anything like Taylor's skill. It was clear that she and the camera loved one another and had since her childhood when she first stood before it. To that point, by the way, he'd carefully referred to her as "Miss Taylor."

We talked on pleasantly till 2:30 when Richard suggested lunch. We abandoned the secretary and his friends, and Mario drove us a few miles inwards on the Appia to a small restaurant called L'Escargot. We passed through a dark inner room, with much whispering of recognition, as Richard led us onto a vine-covered courtyard. There we ate a long hot delicious lunch (in my calendar I even sketched the table and our relative seats). The calendar also says:

> The talk was of Burton's huge Welsh family—thirteen children, his father a miner with a little Greek and Latin, who drank himself to death ("As I could easily do"); of Dylan Thomas whom he knew from the time he was 8 (his father had seen a poem of Thomas's in a Welsh paper and invited him to stay); of his desire to do a season at the Aldwych [in London] next year— Richard II, III and Falstaff. He talked at length—persuasively and movingly—about his reading of Richard II which he believes genuinely and legitimately different from Gielgud's—with much quoting. A harsh, ironic Richard. Then he began to speak of the Taylor-Burton scandal. His version was that it was entirely the product of coincidence and yellow journalism. "Miss Taylor's husband had decided to leave her some time ago. Coincidentally, he and my wife left Rome on the same day—my wife to put my daughter in school in London. The press leapt and, hot-headedly, I took Miss Taylor out for an evening in town." From the start I felt very unsure about his "version" but I *did* feel great warmth for *him*. He said to Stephen, "Isn't there something that can be done

to clear up all this nonsense in England? After all, I am a serious actor." Stephen suggested a letter to *The Times*; Burton seemed glad at the idea. At one point a waiter brought a card; a woman saying "I need a photograph of you." He answered politely, asking for her address.

At a long table beyond us there was a party of some twenty Italians who, I noticed, paid no attention whatever to Richard. Then midway through lunch I realized that one of them was Marcello Mastroianni—snow white hair for his role in 8½, as I'd learn later. I said nothing about my hunch at the time—Richard was drinking several cognacs atop our Bloody Marys and the wine with lunch; and he talked more about getting on drinking spells for days, though "I hold it well."

We left L'Escargot at about 3:30 and headed straight for Cinecittà. Richard wanted us to see the huge set of the Roman Forum. In the car I mentioned that I thought I'd seen Mastroianni just now. Mario said "Yes—and Mr. Fellini." Richard said "I know Fellini very well." But he hadn't stopped to speak which left me wondering if the natives were avoiding Burton for whatever reason. At the studio the set was indeed colossal and impressive—a very credible place, all the more fascinating in light of the numerous hours I'd spent in its surviving ruins back in town behind us.

As we neared the full-scale reproduction of the ancient rostrum, it occurred to me that—lubricated as he now was—Richard might mount the steps and recite a few Shakespearean lines from Antony's funeral oration for Caesar—"Friends, Romans, countrymen." But the thought proved unworthy of the man. Clearly in the past three hours, he'd been engaged in a very gifted young man's effort to persuade an older visiting poet of his seriousness as an actor and a man; and clearly he'd done so. He was hardly likely now to perform a schoolboy trick, however charming he could have made it. Yet he needed another drink; so we walked to the nearby studio commissary, a remarkably unimpressive hut, for more brandy (I was drinking ginger ale by then).

We talked more of Dylan Thomas, and finally Stephen said how sorry he was not to have seen Miss Taylor. That triggered a long explanation about today's cancellation by the female star. Not only did her contract award her days off when she suffered her period, she had not been able to inform the producer of the commencement of her menses till early this morning (thereby invoking her period clause); so it was too late to cancel the costuming of hundreds of "Nubian slaves" for the day's scene—Cleopatra's arrival in Rome. Thus many more thousands of Fox dollars rushed down the drain. When Stephen and I must have looked appropriately staggered by such power, then with no pause whatever, Richard said "Would you really like to meet her?" Stephen said "Yes, very much." So Richard walked ten feet to a nearby wall phone and dialed a number. It was my delayed realization that, with the right number and a workable finger, you could theoretically phone any of the world's prominent figures.

In three minutes Richard was back. "She said 'Come round if you don't mind me being ugly. I've been in bed. Just give me ten minutes.'" We gave her thirty minutes while Richard had another brandy, and Taylor phoned the commissary to say "Come on, I'm getting nervous waiting." So we headed for her villa and somehow Vivien Leigh entered our talk. Richard spoke of her very admiringly and affectionately and—referring to her long and now troubled marriage with Olivier—he said "Poor darling, she's carried that marriage on her back for twenty years." It was a markedly different view from the prevailing sense that an eminently sane Olivier had borne Leigh and her breakdowns with devoted patience for years.

I couldn't gauge the distance accurately, but it didn't seem to me that Taylor's villa was especially near Richard's. Wherever, we approached the door and entered without knocking. Onward down a short hallway; and there she was, seated in a small room with an older man, perhaps her agent. She greeted us gladly from her chair (I think there was a mild kiss between the two stars); then she stood and led us into the living room—not as large or as striking as Richard's. Once there, she took a seat on a long sofa and motioned Stephen and me to sit on her right and her left. By then I'd had a chance to confirm the obvious—"She was very beautiful—short and in an orange and lemon figured house-gown, low necked. Her hair was long and worn loose with only a horn bandeau."

Richard said "Mr. Price is another Welshman." Taylor said to me "Do you have any Jewish blood?" (She'd converted to Judaism with a prior husband; and as long as I had black hair, I was often thought to be Jewish.) When I said "No," Stephen told her that he did—he was one fourth Jewish. Then another small American factotum entered with gins-and-tonic and promptly vanished. Richard said "Show them what I gave you"; and she drew from her bosom a gold—apparently ancient—coin with Cleopatra on one side, Antony on the other. By then Richard had plainly abandoned his earlier extremely cool definition of their relation.

Thereafter the two main topics of conversation were money and Taylor's nearly fatal case of pneumonia several years earlier. Shortly after we were seated with our drinks, Richard said to Taylor "Tell them how much you're making, love." She frowned—"That's vulgar, Richard. You tell them." With the grinning incredulity of a poor miner's son, Burton proceeded to lay out the phenomenal sums she'd ultimately make, concluding with "She's making fifty thousand dollars a week" (some $300,000 by current value). When he'd spun out his whole gold-encrusted fascination for us, Taylor said "But in the end, I'll simply make thirty thousand a year; isn't that what everyone makes—after taxes, I mean?" The pneumonia story—which Burton urged her to tell us, like a teacher goading his prize pupil—concerned a siege of the illness she suffered during the first attempt to film *Cleopatra* in England. She'd been abed in her hotel suite when her vital signs suddenly plunged; and London's best pneumatologist was summoned—Sir Someone-or-Other who also attended the Queen's chest. I'll call the doctor Sir Hartley and add that my calendar says "suddenly she was speaking with great intensity of the point at which she died for fifteen seconds or so, her husband Eddie Fisher had knelt to pray and, in desperation, the doctor began pummeling her breasts, then gouging her eyes to make her gasp for air. She looked up to Burton and said "Can I tell them what I said, Richard?" "Of course, they're grown men." "I said 'Why don't you fuck off?'" The word was a little more startling then than now, and none of us quite laughed.

Stephen asked if she remembered how it felt to be dead. "She said it was a great relief after the awful struggle of trying to breathe. And she dreamt." One of us asked if she remembered the dreams. "Yes. But I've never told anyone this. I dreamt I was with Mike. My late husband [Michael Todd]." By then Stephen and I were fairly caught in her toils—not that I doubt the awfulness of Taylor's plight, but she was after all a resourceful actress. More drinks arrived and soon somehow we were talking about the South. Stephen asked if she wasn't Southern. She reminded him of her birth in Hampstead (Taylor had been born in London in 1932 to American parents), but said that she'd played more than one Southern role and asked me if there was a role for her in my novel. When I said "Not this one, I'm sorry to say," she asked me please to write her one—she was after all thirty, and "the scripts will thin out soon." She also said that she'd never visited the South but would like to—"I'm certainly never going back to California." When I asked, she told me she'd been coached in her Southern accent—and a good one it was—by the novelist Speed Lamkin from Louisiana. I thought that Vivien Leigh had got even better coaching at the hands of Susan Myrick from Georgia, though of course I didn't say it (I recalled reading an interview with Taylor not long before our meeting. She was asked what she wanted to be when she was a little girl, and she said "Vivien Leigh").

Around then Taylor's children returned from their day at school—were there two of them?—and Richard sat with them on the floor, joining in their play. Then came the climax of my time with the small great lady. By then I'd had way more than my daily quotient of drinks; and in a silent gap in our conversation, I was gazing at the amateurish painting of a woman hung over the mantel. I assumed the picture was something that came with the rented villa; and when Elizabeth (as she'd then asked to be) asked how I liked it, I said "I can't say much for it, I'm afraid." She said "Oh really? It's my favorite portrait of myself." I gazed a moment longer and then began the descent into potential danger which easily accompanies excessive gin. I said "You? That doesn't look like you. It doesn't even look like a beautiful woman." I was bold enough at that point to turn and face those violet eyes that, by then, truly seemed to care for my opinion. So I rose to my reckless climax—"It doesn't even look like a human being."

She took a remarkably effective silent beat while my gauche error bored in upon me. Then she said "You didn't think I was a human being? You don't think if you'd lived in this world since you were five years old, you'd be a human being?" As the awful honesty of her self-knowledge finally reached me, she brought her left hand down on my right knee. All my walking life, I'd had a trick knee; it could easily kick outward when slapped. And so it did now, right into the glass coffee table parked before us. The table shuddered forward toward Richard and the children; and I half expected Elizabeth to call out the dogs. But no, Elizabeth took another awesome beat; then gave her best high raucous laugh—*washerwoman's arms and a fishwife's laugh*—and reached for her drink.

Not long after, Stephen looked at his watch and said that we really must leave. Both Elizabeth and Richard pressed us to stay. She said "We'll rustle up a true Egyptian feast." I thought "Splendid." But Stephen reminded us we had tickets for the opera at eight (it was maybe six by then). So like a pair of hapless fools, we rose to leave, followed by Cleopatra and her Antony—or a live man and woman more powerful, in economic power at least, than the real ancient lovers had ever been—and her two beautiful children, all murmuring objections to our departure.

Mario drove us back to the Milton, we ate a quick supper, and left on foot for the opera. The plan was to hear Bellini's *I Puritani*. More than once I'd heard Maria Callas's grand early recorded performance but had never seen it onstage (the opera was seldom done then in England or the States). Once there, we were ushered to seats on the very front row of an upper balcony. There was no knee-room for Stephen's long legs, and my own not-often-triggered fear of heights was soon engaged by an irrational but strong sense that the entire crowded balcony might suddenly execute a slight tip forward and pour me out onto the orchestra seats far below. Neither of us mentioned our problems till the first intermission (following a good deal of less than spectacular singing). When we stood and confessed our reservations, Stephen offered a simple solution—"Let's leave." We left with no regrets.

That crowded day in Rome was May 10, and the calendar concludes forever with that detailed description of the afternoon with Burton and Taylor. Was I then a starry-eyed celebrity hound to have written up the meeting so fully? After all, several dinners with Cyril Connolly and Stephen Spender no doubt produced considerably more interesting conversation, none of which I recorded. But then in the previous six years, I'd participated in many such talks and had recorded none of them, just as I'd detailed no meetings with other intellectual and theatrical friends. I'm mildly puzzled, then, at discovering how much ink I spent on Taylor and Burton.

Yet in explaining myself—at age twenty-nine—to myself today, I conclude that the film stars were not merely outrageously notorious in the media of the time, they were also distinctly gifted in that brief moment of all our lives and of course they were physically magnetic to the eyes—he in his rough-hewn, intensely masculine yet consciously seductive way; she in her unadorned near perfection at age thirty (there was a minute depression, the literal size of a pinprick, in one of her cheeks). Lifelong consumer of human beauty that I was then—and still am—I was almost never in the company of such gods; and had I spent an entire evening with the Oliviers, say, or Alain Delon, I hope I'd have taken similar pains to record the facts.

Since my calendar shuts down in early May '62, I can note that my passport shows I returned to London on the eleventh and departed from Southampton for New York on the eighteenth—a final English week then to account for and strangely I preserve very few memories of those days. Did Stephen and I return to Heathrow on the same flight? Did I stay in London, at the Craxtons' or at Matyas and Sofia's? Back in Oxford, did I stay at Matyas's; or did Merton lend me its guest room? Did I give further interviews in connection with the publication of my novel? To all those questions, I can only shake an unknowing head. Is it memory overload from such a busy, and generally happy, year? Or a lack of further memorable experiences?

I do, though, recall three things. I know that I visited Wally in

Merton once again. Since our last meeting, he'd met a Norwegian woman his age. She was in England to study nursing, her name was Sissel, and she was the first human being with whom I'd seen the self-possessed Wally plainly in love. I still possess a snapshot in which Sissel is gazing downward, long blond hair pulled back, with Wally turned toward her in patent adoration. And I know that Ben Holman and I returned to Covent Garden once more for a full evening—the Royal Ballet performed its new version of Stravinsky's *Rite of Spring* with décor by Sidney Nolan, and then on May 16 Wally came down from Oxford and he, Ben, and I saw a performance by Rudolf Nureyev in something astonishing—but what? In those frigid Cold War days, the young dancer had eluded his Soviet guards and defected, sensationally, eleven months earlier at the Paris airport. He'd not yet committed himself, as he soon would, to join the Royal Ballet for much of the rest of his life—his long partnership with Margot Fonteyn would be especially memorable—so the performance which Ben and I saw was by way of being one of several initial glimpses offered by a pantherine boy of enormous talent to potential future audiences and employers.

What I saw that warm May evening, from a stage-right balcony, was stupefying in its physical daring and achievement—Nureyev reached for nothing that eluded his grasp—but Ben was more suspicious than I of the potential endurance and depth of such a dashing Tartar head and miraculous body (the next decade would prove Ben wrong, as I'd learn when I saw Nureyev some fifteen years later in the Canadian Ballet's *Sleeping Beauty* at the Metropolitan in New York). Finally I know that Ben and I again spent several nights together at the Regent Palace Hotel off Piccadilly, where I'd stayed with Jim Griffin in December '55. I saw my friends at Chatto and Windus, then took Ben to lunch with Stephen.

After that—with no self-pity—Ben told me of his plan to stay on in London, teaching wherever he could find dance classes. I suspected that his English choreographer would never relent and welcome him back. Ben suspected the same and it proved to be the case. I sensed that his already strong degree of loneliness, at such an early age, would only intensify; but I saw the futility of urging a return to the States. I think he had no siblings, and he didn't seem close to his parents. Like every successful dancer I've subsequently known, he was utterly determined to do his own will, even headstrong in his aim; and that force sustained him for at least as long as we stayed in touch.

Three years after our British meetings, Ben would visit me once more—in my newly purchased home in Durham—but then we slowly lost all contact (even Google can no longer find him). At the time of our last meeting, his involvement in Subud had not only continued but had led him to change his first name to William. He was likewise preparing to travel far, and in several directions, hunting the spiritual gifts of the discipline. By then he was twenty-two years old and seemed to have abandoned dance. He appeared to be on a path much like the many paths taken by my students and young friends of the Sixties. I hope it led him onward to some good haven—I thought he deserved that. In those two weeks with Ben, I learned things that would go on changing me for a long time to come.

On May 18 I took a train once more to Southampton and boarded the *France*. The fourth-largest liner then at sea, it had been afloat—as a fully fitted ship—for only four months. Like the *United States* its interiors were limited to metal construction (since wood violated fire laws) and were not notably elegant; but the lean lines and ceilings of the various rooms, small or large, were imaginative throughout. My first-time private cabin was still in tourist class—Deck B, Cabin

168. And with a whole stateroom and bath to myself, I moved out past the Isle of Wight (which at Oxford was often called the Izzle of Widget) with my hopes of at least a brief waterborne attachment.

On westward then through five days and nights in unblemished spring weather, I slept long nights (and long afternoon naps) in a good-sized private cabin so I wasn't at the mercy of early-rising, late-sleeping, or snoring mates. The ship was much the nicest, physically, I was ever on. I read the whole of Tolstoy's *Resurrection* and thereby completed my traversal of his fiction. And I read *Under the Volcano* (which I admired very much but didn't like), Rimbaud, and me (trying to think of questions to ask Fred Coe). Also I did a good deal of thinking about the new novel and made a lot of notes for it. I ate the superb cuisine, those three vast meals every day, and drank the good wine. I sat up late in several bars, drinking unusual amounts. I even took the proffered tours of the engine room with its giant turbines and the captain's bridge. But on the last morning, I was forced to laugh at my own delusion—I'd spent every horizontal hour alone, not even so much as a furtive embrace upright against a bulkhead. In fact, I can no longer recall meeting anyone, though surely I must have (it was my sixth and, so far, final crossing by sea). In my inevitable solitary walks round deck, I must have thought about a number of imminent problems—finding living quarters in the Durham countryside, writing the remaining long story for my volume (I'd yet to write a word of the text, though I had the idea), and locating the one great desire I'd yet to fulfill (and that somehow still seemed possible): chancing on a man I could love and be loved by, in close proximity from here to the grave.

My single memorable shipboard event came on the last morning. We approached Manhattan fairly early—more cloudless sunlight—and as we neared the Statue of Liberty, hundreds of my fellow passengers moved to the port-side rail and watched the great

Lady heave into view, herself a French gift to the harbor and as solemn in demeanor as most of the crew had been throughout our crossing. I've often heard of passengers feeling welcomed by the Statue of Liberty, but I've wondered how closely they examined her face as their ship slid past. Or is it because I'm American by birth that, the three times I've passed her on return voyages—and always through glad tears—I've seen her dauntingly grave (even grim) face, her upraised arm and torch, as far more nearly a challenge than a welcome? And far more than the moving first-person declarative speech that concludes Emma Lazarus's sonnet, preserved in her base, Liberty has seemed to say *Can you enter here and employ with honor, throughout your stay, the fact of liberty: more freedom than any other country has offered in the history of the human race but a solemn freedom?*

Here I stood on the near edge of thirty (I'd pass that milestone in under nine months). A man in excellent health, with no wife or children or committed partner, a mother who required little financial support (though my capital was now more hefty than ever), a brother about to be supported by the U.S. Navy, no house presently arranged for my ongoing residence, and a second book two-thirds complete in manuscript—what would I do with this much liberty again? With the sense of gentle rolling which a sea voyage awards me for days after landing, I came down the French ramp onto native ground with Liberty's question troubling my mind as never before. I'd left home almost exactly ten months ago with the main intention that was stifled on my first night in England—the hope of an intensified relation with Matyas. And while he and I, and the woman he married midway through my stay, had established a new kind of friendship, Matyas and I never again reforged the particular bond we'd shared in those few months of '58. I'd left home with plans to complete at least a second book—the few short stories I'd mostly completed in my first Oxford stint and as many new stories as I could invent. I'd managed only to continue revising the old stories with a semi-mad hyperattentiveness; and I'd added a single story, "Uncle Grant." The volume of stories, then, needed one long new story or several shorter ones; and I was due to teach full-time again in under four months. In the face of my first-night disappointment—which oddly never became a heartache—I well understood I'd had a fine year, rich in the kinds of friendship native to the English of those years—*exclusive* to them in my experience (and all those kinds of friendship seemed to me to spring from a single desire: a steady need for relations of mutual dependence that, while they were cooler than sexual bonds, were likely to be far more loyal, and for longer stretches of time, than all but a very few physical relations).

So apart from greeting my mother and brother, my Durham friends and my Warrenton kin, I'd need to haul ass to Durham, very soon then, and find new lodgings (such a reunion with family and colleagues may have been my main reason for coming home two months sooner than I'd planned). The process of arrival in NY was the most harrowing yet: I walked off the ship at ten a.m. It wasn't until twelve that I had rounded up my six pieces of luggage—the helpful porters had filed them away under three different letters of the alphabet, over the space of a quarter mile of pier. In those days, many of them were clearly involved in profit-sharing deals with the brawny porters and flaks from shipping companies. The customs man would often break the lock on your trunk as you stood there helpless with your key (that had already happened, expensively, on my return in '58). Then with your trunk semi-ruined, he'd take a cursory look at the upmost layer of your belongings, then indicate with an impatient thumb that the shipping clerk who was standing by could now be paid to repair your lock and get you quickly out of customs' ruinous way. The one happy thing, on this second return I drew a very pleasant customs inspector who only made me open my shaving kit. My small trunk was spared, but I still had to yield it to Railway Express for delivery to Raleigh.

Outside in the mob of liberated passengers, many of them baffled in their first sight of metropolitan America, I was pleased again to exercise my hard-won Manhattan skills in hailing a cab—"149 East Sixty-first please." The address was the apartment of Samuel Barber, the American composer. I'd not yet met him; but Stephen had seen him recently, shortly after Barber had read my novel. They were old friends—Sam had long ago set to music one of Stephen's Spanish Civil War poems—and Sam had expressed an interest in talking with me about collaborating on a possible libretto. Rudolf Bing, the imperious director of the Metropolitan Opera, was in the process of commissioning an opera to open the new Met in Lincoln Center in the fall of 1966, a little more than four years from then; Sam, whose *Vanessa* had premiered at the old Met in '58, had been chosen for the honor—and burden—and was in dire need of a new libretto.

Like most lovers of American music, I knew Barber's imposing *Adagio for Strings* but little else from his relatively small but gallant body of orchestral, vocal, and instrumental work. After Stephen delivered the message, I contacted Barber and told him of my arrival time and my hope to stay in New York for several days before heading south. He replied by cable, asking me to come straight from my ship to his apartment in the city. We could have lunch at least. On the quiet tree-lined block of East Sixty-first, I found his entrance, rang the bell for 2B, identified myself to the man's voice that answered, and entered the buzzing door. A small door opened on the second floor as I climbed the stairs; and when I reached the top, a middle-aged man about my height—a little under six feet—

Samuel Barber, a few years after Reynolds first met him. They toyed for a while with collaborating on an opera for Leontyne Price, but Barber eventually opted for Shakespeare as his librettist.

was waiting pleasantly. Sam Barber was then fifty-two years old, slender enough, a likable face (not quite handsome) with searching eyes and a baritone speaking voice that—even if Stephen had not prepared me—suggested a queer propensity.

It was around one o'clock. As I set down my small bag, Sam sped through our immediate options. If I cared to move fast, we could have a quick Dubonnet here, go out for lunch, then head quickly north to 155th Street where the American Academy of Arts and Letters was staging its annual spring prize day—Eudora Welty would be there to award the gold medal for fiction to William Faulkner who'd waited a long while to get it. He was sixty-four and the Nobel committee in Stockholm had tapped him twelve years before his native Academy had seen fit to gild him. So I could see Eudora for the first time in years; maybe I could even shake hands with a man I'd known to be a genius since I first read *The Sound and the Fury* at Harvard summer school in '54, a genius who nonetheless hardly warmed my heart.

I washed up, drank my first ever glass of Dubonnet while Sam questioned me in detail about the *France* (he often went to Europe in ships). By the time we headed to lunch, I felt that I liked him, though the feeling was jostled as Sam made an unkind remark about Stephen while hailing a taxi. We crossed town and took our seats in an enjoyably ludicrous restaurant near Rockefeller Center. It was called the Forum of the Twelve Caesars (the ice buckets were mock gladiator's helmets). The food was good but not overwhelming for someone only two weeks from Rome and a few hours from the *France*. I'd expected Sam to launch soon into some discussion of an opera; but we talked on about a good deal else, including his keen-eyed reading of my novel (I'd soon learn how widely Sam read in contemporary fiction).

The Academy was swarming when we got there—its famous members (writers, painters, sculptors, architects, and composers), their partners and guests, and the hundreds of assorted fans whom I'd later learn were avid attendants at any open function on 155th Street at Riverside Drive. The first hand I shook near the door was the poet Richard Wilbur's; and then Sam guided me into a room where I spotted Eudora in a bottle-green dress and went straight toward her. At the time she was fifty-three years old, we'd only met a few times in 1955, and now she seemed pleasant but cooler than I remembered—it was my introduction to her shyness in crowds. Older friends came up steadily to greet her, but I had time to notice sadly that she'd developed a spinal problem since our last meeting—what my mother would have called a "widow's hump." When I met other friends of Eudora in forthcoming years, almost no one (but a physician at a party in Nashville) mentioned her problem to me. It was osteoporosis, a then common form of bone weakness in middle-aged women of those years and one that might have been tempered with calcium supplements.

The event was long and hot and rather boring; still, it was nice to see virtually every American poet, novelist, and painter, etc., over thirty-five in one room—old Frost being led round like Oedipus by Lewis Mumford, Marianne Moore in that black velvet toadstool hat, Robert Lowell, St. John Perse with dyed black hair, Aldous Huxley, I. A. Richards. Eventually a bell rang and everyone streamed toward the big auditorium—Sam and Eudora to their places onstage among the other members who sat in chairs on several risers, and I toward a looming balcony on stage right. Our programs identified the members by the numbers of their chairs. I seem to recall finding Georgia O'Keeffe, Virgil Thomson, and Aaron Copland—their faces as recognizable and as mildly unnerving in their breathing grinning reality as Julius Caesar's paralyzed profile on a Roman coin. The very sight of so many artists of such real distinction was my best welcome home, so far at least. In the crowded room, only minutes ago, two or three strangers had actually come up and praised my novel; and while I certainly knew that my chance of occupying a member's chair on that stage was a distant—if not impossible—goal, I was breathing an air that braced me throughout the long award of assorted prizes—a grander form of high-school commencement. Huxley, near blind as he was, read a winning brief lecture.

Then very near the end, Eudora stood to read her short and earnest praise of William Faulkner. (I'd come to realize that she admired him past the point of idolatry.) Despite her spinal weakness, she was still a tall woman—all but six feet—and the prior speaker had politely adjusted the microphone for her height and her soft voice. When Faulkner rose to take the medal and thank the Academy, it was easy enough to see he was markedly shorter than Eudora; but he made no effort to adjust the mike. He looked like a mad little briar pipe—dry and dark brown and indescribably distinguished, but bored. He hadn't cracked a smile in the whole two hours, and I can't say as I blame him. He looked down doggedly at his notes, never looked up at the audience, and read his speech toward the lower stem of the mike in his own soft high-pitched Mississippi voice. No one could tell one word from another—not I anyhow (and my ears were sharp then). At the crowded reception, beside the Academy on a tented plaza in late afternoon, I saw Julie Harris who was there to get a medal for Good Speech on the stage. I didn't introduce myself or ask her, "Do you want to be Rosacoke, honey?" but I walked up to her and just stared for long enough to establish that, despite her thirty-six years, she could easily pass for twenty in a film. And what a voice, what a face.

After the reception Sam Barber stepped aside to speak with friends; and I was waiting alone on the curb. I looked uphill some few yards, and there William Faulkner was likewise standing alone. He was nattily dressed, as I'd heard he would be; and his hair was pure white in the warm patch of sun all round him. In fact he was isolated in a column of light, looking straight ahead at a block-sized graveyard immediately across the narrow street—old tombstones shaded by huge trees. He seemed at least as alone as any nearby corpse, so I suddenly thought I'd move up toward him and introduce myself.

I had no notion he'd ever heard my name, but that wouldn't be the point of spending thirty seconds with a man who'd written two or three novels fit to stand with the best in American history. I'd heard of his potential rudeness; so I held back though, and in two more minutes a young fellow came up and moved the great man on uphill toward Broadway. He'd be dead, in an alcoholic's drying-out clinic, in under six weeks from that moment; and a year later I'd learn from a reliable source that he'd actually read *A Long and Happy Life*. What in God's name might he have said to my face if I'd taken my own dare and shaken his hand? When the novel won the William Faulkner Award the next winter, I learned that I'd be the first winner who wouldn't receive the plaque (with the handsome profile I'd just seen) from the hands of Faulkner himself.

Apparently I'd made plans before leaving England to spend a few days at Barber's country house before heading home; so we drove there after leaving the Academy. The house was (a little pretentiously, I thought) called Capricorn and stood on what was then a dirt road a few miles outside the town of Mount Kisco in Westchester County, New York. It had been purchased years earlier by Sam and his longtime partner Gian Carlo Menotti with financial help from Mary Curtis Zimbalist, one of their wealthier patrons. Though I'd heard the house described as a mansion, it was hardly that. In fact when I stayed on the premises, Capricorn itself consisted of a middle-sized living room/dining room, an average-sized kitchen, a servant's room with bath; and modest private quarters at either end for Barber and Menotti—their own beds and bathrooms, their desks and grand pianos.

From the start, the young butler Alfredo De Luise showed me downhill some one hundred yards to a pleasant low guesthouse—a large room and bath, a kitchen alcove. That space communicated with the main house by telephone and was an ideal outpost for friends of the two owners who were there to work, in private or in occasional collaboration. Eleanor Steber, for instance—the distinguished American soprano—had spent several weeks in the guesthouse as she labored with Sam daily on the role of Vanessa for its premiere. Alfredo set my bag down, and at once I phoned Mother and Bill to say I'd be home in another few days. I took a short nap, then changed my sodden shirt for dinner—it had been a hot day.

Sam had asked me to join him at seven in the main house, and I noticed that—when I ordered a gin and tonic—Sam asked Alfredo for a "gin and tonic *senza* gin" (without gin). At the time I thought little about the odd request. I knew that Sam was hard at work on a piano concerto—the first he'd written (and the last, as it turned out)—to be played that September, four months hence, by Robert Browning and the Boston Symphony under Erich Leinsdorf during the festivities for the opening of the new Philharmonic Hall, as it was then called, in Lincoln Center. So I assumed that Sam was temporarily holding back on a number of luxuries. We'd each had smallish lunches at the Forum, and now Alfredo had donned his white jacket to serve us a welcome dinner—pasta, then lamb and fresh corn, then homemade ice cream. All Sam's at-home meals were cooked by Alfredo and his wife, Liliana, an Italian couple in their early twenties whom Menotti had discovered and brought to the States. They were each more than easy on the eyes. In fact Stephen had earlier told me that Alfredo "seemed like a creature made of light," quiet but luminous.

As Sam and I ate and talked, several things became explicit. He was indeed hard at work, and he always worked here in the country whenever possible. Menotti was in Italy, managing his annual festival of the arts in Spoleto, and wouldn't return before fall ("if then"—there was clearly some edge on the phrase). Sam's young friend Manfred Ibel was in his native Germany but would be back here soon. He stayed in a cubicle immediately off Sam's room, so the guesthouse was free for the entire summer; I was welcome to stay as long as I liked. Since I'd yet to find new quarters, the idea was instantly appealing. I could head home briefly to see the family, then drive back to Capricorn after maybe a month's work on my story. Manhattan was an hour away by train for the several articles and interviews that Atheneum had already mentioned in connection with my novel, and Sam had finally—over coffee—mentioned his libretto needs.

Any new opera would star the American soprano Leontyne Price. I'd heard her in the famous revival of *Porgy and Bess* during my junior year at Duke (friends and I had driven up to see Duke play Army in football at the old Polo Grounds; and after a fully disabling auto collision on Riverside Drive—a sudden rear-end crash—we managed to attend *Porgy* at the Ziegfeld Theatre that night). After *Porgy*, Price had performed as a recitalist more than once, with Sam at the piano. She'd also given striking performances with the NBC Opera on television—*Tosca*, *The Magic Flute*, *Don Giovanni*, and *Dialogues of the Carmelites*. Though she'd been born and reared in Laurel, Mississippi (likewise the home of Blanche DuBois), the fact of Price's black origins had led more than one Deep Southern television station to refuse to run those performances. Undeterred, Price had gone to Europe and succeeded widely—above all in *Aida*—and at last, only a year before my return home, she'd made her debut at the Met in a sensationally received *Il Trovatore*.

No debut since Kirsten Flagstad's in 1935 had been so vociferously welcomed; and now Rudolf Bing and Sam were contemplating a gala opera for the new Met, starring Price of course (and as many other American singers as possible). Then Sam told me two more things. He'd approached other writers with no success—I recall the names of Thornton Wilder and Tennessee Williams—and he'd appreciate my not mentioning the plan until further notice. He'd yet to accept a formal commission from the Met; and most interestingly, both he and Leontyne hoped to develop an opera in which she'd have yet another role, besides Aida, which she could sing as a specifically black woman. Yet given the still intense ongoing civil rights movement in the nation, Leontyne would not want to appear in a story concerned with white-black violence of any sort.

I asked if Sam—or Miss Price, as I then called her—had any ideas yet for a possible story. No, they didn't—nor did anyone else he'd consulted. He'd asked me to visit in the hope that—Southerner as I was, in my life and my fiction—I'd think of the ideal story: white and black and no bloodshed. At the moment I went entirely blank but told him of my generally enthusiastic interest in opera since the early days of high school and of how compelling the prospect of working with him and Miss Price could well be. Then Sam repeated the fact of his immersion in the piano concerto and renewed the invitation to stay in the guesthouse as long as I liked. I could write uninterruptedly during the day; and we could talk over meals, if nothing more, till he finished the concerto. At that point he had no notion whatever for a final movement and was clearly growing concerned.

I very much wanted to see my family and to anchor myself for the forthcoming year of teaching; but the whole summer lay before me, and the prospect of coming back to Capricorn in the hopes of completing my own book of stories in such likable surroundings and establishing an acquaintance with Sam that might eventually lead to the text for an opera was too good to refuse out of hand (I took it that I'd now been invited to cooperate in the matter). At the end of less than a full day with Sam then, I thanked him and said Yes, I'd like to return here soon; and I'd like to commence thoughts of a libretto.

I also dined, in the city, with Earl McGrath—an energetic and often hilarious assistant to Fred Coe, the man who'd purchased a film option on my novel. Coe was a native of Alligator, Mississippi and had been among the most imaginative of directors in the early days of TV drama and had recently produced his second theatrical film, a successful version of William Gibson's play *The Miracle Worker* (the first was *The Left Handed Gun* with Paul Newman as Billy the Kid). *The Miracle Worker* memorably dramatized the brutal childhood of the deaf-mute Helen Keller and her breakthrough into calm as she began to comprehend the notion of communicative language when Annie Sullivan was hired to teach her. Coe was away from New York at the time of my spring return from Britain (I'd meet him later and would like him). Meanwhile McGrath did his best to convince me of Coe's serious interest in my story and his explicit determination to make it the subject of his next film. McGrath also took me to the first Broadway production of Edward Albee's *Who's Afraid of Virginia Woolf?*, the most powerful modern play I'd seen since Carson McCullers's very different *The Member of the Wedding* in 1950.

In the end I did give the option to Coe, though I hadn't yet talked with him himself. But I had had long talks with McGrath, who appeared to have done most of the advance work; and I was convinced of what I had needed to be convinced of—that Coe, if he could get the backing (and of course there was a real possibility that he couldn't), would make a dignified and honest try.

As I came toward the end of my first New York visit as a newly successful novelist—the book had been on the *Times* bestseller list for several weeks—I began to wonder if I felt in any sense a different man from the one who'd left here for Europe the previous year. In retrospect I'd say that the chief difference was in my new state of considerable nervous elation. Like many young writers, I'd worked for so long, in such uncertainty and relative penury; and now I had not only the encouragement of old colleagues who'd liked my work in manuscript for years, I also had a rapidly rising stack of enviable reviews and the knowledge that my agent and publisher now were receiving a good deal of critical and commercial affirmation of their own gambler's trust in me.

I likewise seemed, in Sam Barber, to be acquiring a rousing opportunity to write something other than fiction. And my family and my small circle of intimates could turn to me now without the suspicion that their friend was little else but another harmless fool, pen and paper in hand (young writers, without a published book, can feel awkwardly suspended in uncertainty). I knew I had light-years to go to build my own house of fiction—and whatever other forms of words I'd employ—but at least I'd started.

I'd phoned home often enough to know that Mother was now puzzled at my ongoing absence. I'd landed nearly two weeks ago. Was something wrong; when could they expect me? Would I fly down or take the usual train? Her voice was still the same young voice. She was fifty-seven; but despite some forty years of smoking, she'd never lost the sound of a young girl's eagerness that was—and would be, first and last—her strongest trait, the gift she offered to all her loved ones (and a good many strangers) almost every day I knew her. I could hardly justify, even to myself, more immediate time

To
Reynolds,
with warm
affection,
Leontyne

The great American soprano Leontyne Price. Even more than Kirsten Flagstad or Marian Anderson (both of whom he venerated), she was Reynolds's most admired vocal artist and, in time, a close personal friend.

in a guesthouse in rural Westchester where the only sounds—but birdsong and civil conversation—were generated by the searching hands of a great composer on a concert grand in his private study (the nearest room from the main house to the guesthouse where I was making more and more elaborate notes going nowhere with the novel I contemplated).

There continued to be temptations to stay. One day Erich Leinsdorf, the conductor of the Boston Symphony who'd lead his players and the solo pianist in the finished concerto in early September, came for lunch with Sam and me—an Austrian American whom I felt I'd like if I had a longer chance (he was full of good jokes). The pianist himself—John Browning, an American from Utah—was exactly my age and came to Capricorn for more than one weekend. He was easy to be with out by the pool, though increasingly edgy at the realization of Sam's near-blockage in the final movement. And all of us were cared for with precise and smiling detail by Alfredo and Liliana, whose grace was all but speechless and far more beautiful than ours.

Nothing, however, made Sam's world seem as tempting as a particular luncheon during my first stint with him. Sam at his own best appeared, in full, on the day when we drove to New York for lunch with Florence Page Kimball, the famous voice teacher, and her star pupil Leontyne Price (despite her married history, Florence Kimball seemed often to be called "Miss Kimball," as older married women in the South were frequently called "Miss So-and-so"). I can come near to dating the meeting when I recall Price's saying, shortly after her arrival, that she'd just sung *Butterfly* and that Fausto Cleva, the conductor, "has almost convinced me that 'Un bel dì' is not my aria." The Met's archives record that such a performance occurred on tour in Detroit on May 23, five days after my return to the States.

Sam and I reached Miss Kimball's apartment a quarter hour before Price; and I had a brief chance to register her teacher's warm face, beneath white hair, atop a short thin frame (she was then seventy-four years old, and her wealthy husband had been dead for many years). She herself had been the pupil of the great Polish soprano Marcella Sembrich and had sought a career in her youth as a recitalist. Then she'd turned to teaching, eventually at Juilliard where, in the early Fifties, she encountered Leontyne Price who'd just come north via Wilberforce College in Ohio. If no other pupil established Florence Page Kimball's name in the annals of eminent voice teachers, Price did—indelibly—and for the remainder of Miss Kimball's life, the soprano remained close to her teacher.

As we continued standing, I noticed a small dining table set with four places. Good, there'd be no one but the three of us and Miss Price. Then the bell rang and in she came. I've mentioned the degree of her overwhelming American success at that point—she'd already received one of the ultimate media accolades (the cover of *Time* magazine); and she was only thirty-five years old. At the start she kissed Miss Kimball and Sam, shook my hand, and at once commented on our shared surname. Then for a while she seemed a little drawn back, though hardly divaesque as we sat and took our glasses of champagne from a maid in regulation black and white attire. During my previous months in England, I'd had little chance to follow the news on Leontyne's second year at the Met; but on our drive to the city, Sam had filled me in.

Leontyne had opened the season in October, with Richard Tucker, in Puccini's *La Fanciulla del West*. Reviews of the performance—her first as Minnie, "The Girl of the Golden West"—confirm her success. A week later she began a second performance of the role and completed the first act with no apparent problem. Near the end of Act Two, however, trouble struck. It was clear that Leontyne was undergoing a singer's darkest nightmare—she was losing her voice onstage. She managed to speak her way through the remainder of the act. (She said later "When I started to speak the words, I was forced to add something in place of song. This time there was an accent and a meaning to the words that I never had before.") In any case, her standby Dorothy Kirsten rushed to the Met and completed the performance. Apparently a combination of a viral infection and the exertions of recent months had taken a serious toll. Leontyne sang four other performances of the role that season, in New York and on tour; then spent considerable time, resting at her parents' home in Mississippi and her own in New York.

She was back now, though, singing on the Met's spring tour. And obviously none of us brought up the season's low point as we were called to table. I recall the remainder of lunch as high fun. Leontyne was then spending a good part of her summers in Rome, recording for RCA Victor; and Sam called on me to tell my story of the recent afternoon with Burton and Taylor. It went down nicely and Leontyne appended a footnote—that she'd been in a Roman restaurant not long ago when Taylor's presence, some tables away, was called to her attention. She laughed—"I got out as soon as I could; that place just wasn't quite big enough for the two of us" (perhaps an unconscious revelation of the degree to which, in Rome still, a famous opera singer could effortlessly rival a film star).

Even before then I'd had a chance to look at her closely—a classic opera singer's frame: not remarkably tall but upright and sturdy with broad shoulders (no significant fat at all) and the always uncanny freight-elevator diaphragmatic waist that accompanies a large voice—any deep breath gave the appearance of a heavy-grade elevator's descent and rise. Her face was young, lovely and almost unguarded, before fame could leave her wary and sometimes frozen. Today it was highly mobile in its range of responses.

Reynolds interviewing the eminent Wagnerian tenor Lauritz Melchior, who was in Raleigh for a 1951 concert. Reynolds was then editor of his high school newspaper and would soon enter Duke. For him, Melchior and Kirsten Flagstad were never surpassed as the supreme interpreters of Wagner.

Another small glass of champagne—but not for Sam—and our laughter increased. I recall even reaching up at one point and tugging on Leontyne's small black hat for some reason—we were nearing the end of long centuries of lady's hats. She thwarted me gently. "Careful, darling, you'll pull my *wig* off" (it would be awhile before I knew that she wore wigs on virtually all occasions). Before lunch ended, we were claiming close kin; and Leontyne volunteered a phrase that we used between us for years thereafter—"There must have been some hanky panky on the old plantation." She cheered me even more by saying "Where have you *been* all my life?"

In earlier years I'd met the singers Kirsten Flagstad and Elisabeth Schwarzkopf briefly. Marian Anderson had spent part of a morning with me when I was fifteen and was still living in Raleigh, well on my way to having a sizable collection of first-class recordings by the great singers of the twentieth century, living and dead (they were my equivalent of stellar athletes—which of course they are, among other things—and no, I have no idea at all why many queer boys share the love of great voices). And I, with my student colleagues from our high-school paper, had interviewed the jovial and candid Lauritz Melchior in his Raleigh hotel suite before a local concert. Devoted almost entirely to the operas of Wagner, still no tenor in modern operatic history seemed greater then than Melchior—and none does yet, perhaps none *as* great as he—but in his suite in the Sir Walter Hotel, he spent an easy forty-five minutes with four teenagers and posed for funny pictures with us all while he told us funny stories (I still recall his answer when I asked him about the most embarrassing moment of his stage career, and he gave us a detailed account of losing the suspender-grip on his chain-mail trousers in Act Two of *Tristan* and having to convey to Isolde, through grimaces and hand gestures, that she must take over the active romance during their impassioned love duet—there was no way he could stand without losing his pants).

And here I was now, in full manhood, joking over lunch with a woman only a little older than I, one who'd eventually be honored as the greatest Verdi soprano in the reach of memory as well as the mistress of a handful of roles by Mozart, Puccini, and Strauss—not to mention Gershwin. That further bolstered her claim to possessing one of the two or three most beautiful soprano voices in memory, a voice deployed furthermore with profound intelligence and a conscientious care that would preserve its beauty well past the usual age at which a woman's voice begins to decay. (Menopause and even monthly periods can strongly affect female voices.)

When lunch was done and we moved back toward the living-room chairs, with no fake shyness Sam went to the piano, introduced what would follow with a sentence or two, then played the moonlit theme from the second movement of his unfinished concerto—it had originated in a flute piece he wrote for his friend Manfred Ibel in 1961. I'd heard it several times before, after dinner at Capricorn; but here with Miss Kimball and Leontyne Price, the passage confirmed its beauty even more deeply. Through the meal, Sam had been quiet, though amused; and Leontyne had paid him no special attention. Now though she was obviously moved and glad to be here with him (for the remainder of his life, her loyalty to him would remain unquestionable; but she did once say to me "Sam is such a *bitch*").

Now I hoped silently that he'd ask her to rise and sing with him one of his *Hermit Songs*—songs they'd premiered and sung together many times from the start of their friendship (she'd recorded the cycle for Columbia). But neither Sam, Miss Kimball, nor Leontyne herself suggested such a thing—nor bumptious I, even with the champagne—and after we'd drunk our thimble of coffee and Sam had asked the ladies to cross their fingers that he'd find a subject for the final movement of his concerto, he and I stood to leave. At the door I kissed both women's cheeks, which they smilingly accepted.

As I recall that meeting, Sam hadn't mentioned his plan for an opera four years from now—how much had he told Leontyne at that point?—so I didn't take the dare I felt like taking: to mention it somehow, however lightly. Maybe it was meant to be a secret all four of us were sharing. Anyhow the past two hours had honed the edge of my own enthusiasm at the prospect, however many hurdles might lie between this afternoon and the stage of the new Metropolitan in September 1966.

I had no way to foresee that in those few years, Sam himself would come to seem fragile in his loneliness and self-doubt; and his relation with Manfred, though it continued, would curdle (I lost touch with Manfred, and I've recently learned that he died of AIDS in Key West in 1992 and that he had, at some point, got married). Leontyne's marriage would end with the discovery of her husband's homosexuality; and given that her powerful voice had already vanished once in the presence of thousands, how might it fail again in the leading role of an opera written to open the new house of the world's most famous company? Further, the unremitting strain of facing life as the first internationally famous black American soprano—especially in the notoriously spiteful backstage corners of opera—would challenge Leontyne's early elasticity.

Still, the ride back to Capricorn, in Sam's top-down convertible was sunlit and warm; and on the way, the time with Leontyne—her clear combination of generous ease, girlish wit and charm with an innate but watchful grandeur—gave me the first feasible idea I'd have for a libretto: Pocahontas on her visit to London in 1616 (the year of Shakespeare's death) when her white husband, John Rolfe, from Jamestown introduced her to King James and Queen Anne;

and the poet Ben Jonson welcomed her to Britain with a masque, "The Vision of Delight."

Admittedly my libretto would center upon a woman with no European blood, though not of African descent, and would have ample opportunities for both intimate feeling and the spectacle traditionally featured in operas composed for festive openings. And perhaps the fact that my nearest cousins—Marcia and Patricia Drake—were direct descendants of Pocahontas on their mother's side (they were, demonstrably, among the famous Indian princess's eighth-great-granddaughters, a kinship I greatly envied in our childhood) would help me construct a text that might even fire a brain as reluctant as Sam's now seemed. I knew that in the course of her visit to England, Pocahontas was suddenly confronted with John Smith, a man whom she likely loved in her early life and whom she's long since been told was dead. Her recorded response to his sudden reappearance, and her immediate action, were powerfully moving—a scene which, alone, would have refuted Sam's later absurd response when he told me that Garson Kanin had previously suggested the Pocahontas idea but that, for him, "Indians onstage always seem funny somehow."

So with Sam's continued invitation to return for a summer's work downhill at his guest cottage—and every intention to accept—in early June I packed my now exhausted clothes and boarded a southbound Seaboard train in Penn Station. It was still the old Penn Station, the country's grandest enormous building, soon to die— incredibly—beneath the wrecker's ball. I booked a private compartment (further benefits of a little new money); and I surely spent the next ten hours in much-needed sleep and reexamined memory— more than half in dreams in which I saw myself as a blurred figure in the middle distance, a figure toward whom I could launch questions no one yet had asked, much less answered.

*   *   *

Back at home I found Mother and Bill in mostly good shape. My only surprise with Mother was the discovery that she promptly resisted my hope of using some of my sudden new money to repair a few obvious needs in our Raleigh house—a new roof, paint, new steps to replace a rotting outdoor staircase. I sensed a perhaps unconscious symptom of her age in the fact that her resistance to change seemed to represent chiefly a refusal of the displacements of change in her quarters (Bill was now a cheerful twenty-one and a student at Duke; and except for summer visits, he and I had left Mother essentially alone for the first time since her marriage in 1927).

When I began to face the prospect of new living quarters in the Durham countryside, I paid a visit to my old landlords out on the edge of the Duke Forest—Henry and Lannie May who'd maintained me (at an unchanging forty-five dollars per month's rent) in their house-trailer for my first three years of teaching. I was surprised to discover that the friend who'd rented the premises when I left had moved out soon thereafter and that the Mays had kept the place empty on the chance that I'd wish to resume residence on my return (the rent would, incredibly, remain the same). Small and inadequately heated as the house-trailer was, its excellent memories and instant availability were overwhelmingly tempting. Without further thought of paying higher rent to find a larger, more comfortable apartment or house, I agreed to rejoin my old landlords, however briefly. Their surrounding pond, woods, and strawy fields made up to me quickly for any remembered inconveniences.

Trips to Macon and Warrenton, my family roots, likewise offered the same old pleasures and reassurances of food, stories, and atmosphere; and it was a great comfort to discover that, if any aunt, uncle, cousin, or old friend disliked or resented any aspect of *A Long and*

Happy Life, they kept the fact to themselves and expressed considerable liking for the book. A few of them saw agreeable resemblances
between one or more of my fictional characters and themselves
or their family relations—resemblances that I generally hadn't
intended or suspected—but, as ever with my country kin, I kept my
thoughts to myself (on the enduring principle which says Do Nothing to Discourage Their Candor).

In my absence in England, my brother had used my 1955 Volks-
wagen. Though it was now seven years old, with 79,000 miles,
the roller-skate-sized car ("Hitler's car," alas) was still in its apparently indestructible state of energy and perky reliability; but having
acquired unexpectedly cheap housing, I began to think of a new car
at the very least. Sam Barber was driving a recent Mercedes sports
car. My own taste was for something a little less jaunty (and less
expensive), so I soon visited the Raleigh Mercedes dealer and came
away in a matter of two or three days with a gray Mercedes 220—a
handsome two-door model with sanguinary leather seats and inte-
rior surroundings, white wall tires, FM radio, and a pervading air of
dignified prosperity. Off then, up the then-less-crowded highways,
to Mount Kisco and Capricorn as promised.

On my days back there with Sam, I felt I was coming to see more
clearly the complex compound he was—and perhaps had to be, to
achieve what he'd written since his early twenties when he produced
the mournful string quartet from which he derived, and orches-
trated lushly, the *Adagio for Strings* (a piece which was less famous
then than now but which, Sam soon told me, already earned him
thirty thousand dollars a year). In the late hours we'd spend after
dinner or driving back from a movie in Mount Kisco, he talked a
good deal about his life and work. Despite the fact that his music
had won the early support of conductors such as Toscanini, Kous-
sevitzky, and Bruno Walter, he'd come to feel—in middle age—that

he'd achieved a certain fame and professional respect in numerous quarters and an assured income; yet he was nonetheless scorned as an old-hat and sadly washed-up Romantic by a few of his contemporaries and a great many younger composers who worked entirely within the airless maze of post-Schoenbergian serial principles, the enemy that had seized the whole American castle some years ago. He even pointed out to me one gray afternoon how Menotti's reputation was worse off than his own, though Gian Carlo had the good sense to take himself and his talent off to Spoleto and be handsomely rewarded there.

Sam reiterated his own scorn on more than one occasion as a chief element in what he described as a profound sense of loneliness here in midlife—and lest any reader think that our late-night conversations were fueled in any sense by alcohol, they weren't. Many of Sam's friends considered, years later, that he died an alcoholic. By then I wasn't seeing him; but in the summer I spent long hours with him, he was bone-dry. I'd later learn that his beloved sister had died not long before I met him—and that she died under conditions which Sam may have thought, rightly or wrongly, suggested suicide. Many aspects of our weeks together then may have emerged under her shadow.

In the near aftermath of that death apparently, Sam was steadily avoiding drink—hence all the gin and tonics *senza* gin. I do know however that in the abstemious summer of '62, he was also paying weekly visits to a Manhattan physician who was giving Sam what he—and many other distinguished Americans, including John Kennedy—were then calling "vitamin shots." What Sam's shots were, and whether they contained steroids or amphetamines, I have no idea. I observed, though, that he'd return to Capricorn after a visit to his doctor with considerably renewed vigor but would seem to decelerate fairly rapidly as succeeding days passed.

The other sadness that recurred in our conversations concerned his relation with Menotti. They'd been students together at the Curtis Institute in Philadelphia in the 1930s, had fallen in love, traveled widely in America and Europe before the Second War, and made their entries into the world of serious music at roughly the same time. After some forty years of a fairly idyllic relation (including life together but no overt display of queerdom), they began to move apart—I'm trying here to recall Sam's version of their relation; I never met Menotti.

At that point Sam's own career remained in the less spectacular realm of often-played symphonic music while Gian Carlo's moved decisively onto Broadway stages, with the unprecedented popular success of post-Puccinean operas like *The Medium, The Consul,* and *The Saint of Bleecker Street,* and his moving and hugely successful televised Christmas opera *Amahl and the Night Visitors.* In the face of all that, the two men's commitment to one another slowly weakened—or Gian Carlo's sense of their relation altered. He spent more and more time in Europe; and then, as Sam said, "all these boys" entered their lives—young men (some of them honorable musicians, artists, and actors) who served generally short-term roles as their sexual companions. Yet Sam told me once "The only man I've ever loved is Gian Carlo, and now he's far gone"—far gone despite the fact that Menotti still maintained his American residence at Capricorn.

Short of thirty as I still was, I'd nonetheless heard such stories—or witnessed their enactment more often than not in the world of male relations. Those failures, if failures they were, left me with more than a suspicion that a mutually satisfying long-term relation between two men—in our culture anyhow—was exponentially more difficult than heterosexual marriage, not to mention the prevalent scorn for such attempted unions and the fact that the sexual intimacy which had been at their heart was gravely illegal (I'm speaking now of public opinion in the 1960s). To what degree my own eventual single life may have been influenced by any such early observations, I'll never know; but I'm trying to report my memories honestly. More than forty years after my talks with Sam, the heterosexual divorce rate is itself appallingly high; and I've taught dozens of students who were the psychic victims of their parents' decision to destroy a family.

In the summer of '62, Samuel Barber was in many ways a desolate man, and profoundly depressed despite the fact that his latest partner—the handsome but boisterous Manfred—was returning to Capricorn soon. Many of Sam's friends had found his relation with a rowdy and often tactless Siegfried to be inexplicable. A sample of Manfred's tact surfaced when he took his first look inside my red-lined Mercedes and said "Nice, yes—in Germany we call this 'the butcher's car.'" Yet for a number of reasons I liked Manfred. He was four years younger than I (twenty-five at the time), he was no fool at all—a good flute player, a textbook example of blond German looks, he was generally kind to me; and we often swam together in the pool at Capricorn, laughing till we had to struggle to breathe.

In addition to Sam's sadness, for whatever reasons (as I began to see on this second visit) he also had a hard edge that could suddenly flash out and shock his friends. Of such moments in my own time with him, I recall typically Sam's walking down to the guesthouse toward noon on August 6 to bring me my mail. As I turned to go I told him I'd see him shortly for lunch. As he turned to go, he said "Oh by the way, Marilyn Monroe died last night—a suicide." Like many Americans of my generation I was struck harder than I'd have guessed by the news. I'd admired Monroe from the start when she appeared nude in *Playboy*, my freshman year at Duke; and I said to

Sam "That's *awful.*" Leaving, though, he said "I don't feel the loss of performing artists the way I do when a real creator dies" (as though Monroe's best performances, like hers in *Bus Stop, The Prince and the Showgirl,* and *Some Like It Hot* weren't indelible creations).

After nearly a month, to my surprise, Sam asked me when I planned to leave the guesthouse. I never asked him to explain the question. (His reasons likely involved people who can't now be discussed.) Of the last two weeks at Sam's ten days were happy, though furtive. The last four were pretty tough. My friend Wally at Oxford also wrote from the depths of despair at his friend Sissel's coming departure for Norway. I answered "Do let me say one Very Cynical thing (as I am a Cynical Young Writer)—and it's something I've repeated to myself like a litany these past two months: don't take the Platonic notion of 'This is the *one* person on earth, ever, for me' too desperately."

After some two weeks in the guesthouse, the trip down from New York was amazingly effortless. I just aimed the nose south, once I'd crossed the Hudson at Nyack, and the rest of the time thought about my story. I'd meant to stop for the night with Mike, but about Wilmington, Delaware I suddenly saw the way the story had to go — quite clearly and thrillingly—so I just drove on and on and got to Durham at two a.m.

When classes began in late September, I took up a suggestion from the director of freshman English, and began to teach a small course for first-year men and women who had a demonstrated talent for narrative writing (for nearly a decade more before his retirement, my old teacher and friend Bill Blackburn would continue holding down his own advanced course; and I couldn't think of interloping in any way upon his successful and watchfully guarded ground).

I taught my own group of freshmen for several years; and though only one of them went on to become a professional writer of fiction—and Josephine Humphreys is a very original novelist, as is Anne Tyler whom I'd taught years earlier—several others took up careers in writing poetry and publishing. Otherwise I taught my old literature course, "Representative British Writers," and several other courses that kept me lightly busy for those four months each year in which I was now teaching.

On my return from England, in light of my new (and so far as I could see, unpredictable) prosperity, I'd asked my chairman if I might teach for one semester the following year and take a reduction in salary. He agreed, the reduction wasn't quite fifty percent; so I went on through succeeding years making the same arrangement with various other chairs until—in the early 1970s—the university and I came to a continuing agreement that, for the remainder of my career, one semester would be my teaching load each year and that, in addition, I'd deposit in the Duke Library on a regular basis the manuscripts of all my books and my incoming personal correspondence.

In the English Department of those years, the hard current realities of tenure-track appointments had not solidified; but I can no longer reconstruct the process by which, not many years after my return from England in '62, I was no longer a three-year instructor— I'd quietly become a permanent member of the faculty. My rise through the ranks, however, was a good deal slower; and it was years before I reached the status of a chaired professor, the best rank that the university confers. (Incidentally, when the letter from President Terry Sanford arrived, notifying me of my ascent to the James B. Duke chair, I suspected that a joke was being played by one or more jolly colleagues; and when I glanced up at the date of the letter— April 1, 1977—I *knew* it was a joke. To confirm my doubts, I phoned the president's secretary who cheerfully confirmed that the news

was credible—she'd typed the letter herself and hadn't realized that
the date might trigger doubts. Less happily—it may say something
about academe's susceptibility to normal human rivalry—I received
only a single word of congratulation from my numerous departmen-
tal colleagues, one that came from a man who'd taught me when I
was a sophomore.)

As it soon became clear that my mind was a reliable fiction-
factory, why didn't I retire from teaching and devote all my time
to writing? First perhaps because I'd planned since the age of sixteen to teach and to write. But even more significantly, I'm sure
because I'd quickly come to love teaching—and for numerous reasons that included my colleagues, a parental impulse, and the
opportunity to regularly off-load the mind's fermentation. Back in
my house-trailer and relatively settled back in as a resident American on home turf, I soon got to work on the story that proved
to complete my next volume. The story became the title story of
the collection—*The Names and Faces of Heroes*—and though I
can no longer recall the actual evolution of its basic premise, I
know it's based on an actual event in my boyhood—it dates to the
year 1943 when my father and I drove from Asheboro, our home
then, to Raleigh to hear the famous Southern Baptist preacher,
Dr. George W. Truett. My father had grown up in the Warrenton
Baptist Church (his mother was Baptist, his father Episcopalian),
and he'd read a good many of Dr. Truett's sermons through the
years. He'd even told me once, when I was going through a pre-
adolescent period of wondering about the actual physical appearance of Jesus, that Dr. Truett had actually seen Jesus in a dream.
As I remember, Dr. Truett had killed a friend in a hunting accident; and of course he suffered agonies of remorse. Then Jesus
appeared to Truett, quite clearly, and eased his mind. When I
asked Dad about discovering the likeness for myself, he said that it

would be findable in "student Bibles," though I don't quite recall his saying where I could find one of those treasure troves.

So once Dad suggested the drive to Raleigh when I was ten, I was more eager to go than I might otherwise have been. Maybe Dr. Truett would tell us something about Jesus' appearance; maybe he'd even had pictures drawn—like police identity pictures—that he would show us from the platform. Well, of course not. I was doomed to disappointment on that score; otherwise I recall almost nothing about the trip—except for the fact that it was one of the rare times when I was alone with my father for the better part of a whole day.

Dad was a kind and often funny man, and there was never any doubt that he loved both me and my younger brother as well as our mother, but he gave few of the standard demonstrations of his feelings. He usually came home at five thirty from work, took a brief nap in his chair, then we dined together without excessive talk. I can recall a single time when Dad went out and pitched a baseball to me (I was wearing the nicely used glove we'd bought from a newspaper ad), but after twenty minutes of failure on my part, it was clear that my catching abilities were nearly nonexistent; and we seldom renewed the embarrassing attempt. And never once did he wind up on the floor with either of us boys in laughing hijinks.

Yet there was something so mysteriously magnetic in his general silence around the house that the mere mention of a possible drive together to Raleigh had me excited. The trip actually occurred and still lingers with me as the happiest time Dad and I ever spent together (he died when I was twenty-one). So the story I wrote in the late summer and fall of '62 was a belated attempt to capture the magical aura of Dad and me at our best (as a very young child, I'd been increasingly crucial in his surrendering an alcohol addiction). I haven't reread the long story in years, but a number of strangers' responses have suggested to me that some of the magic is conveyed to a sympathetic reader.

When the stories were completed, I shipped the manuscript off to Diarmuid Russell, my agent; and my editor at Atheneum, Hiram Haydn, was pleased to set the book on its slow way down the production line at Atheneum. Meanwhile I went on with my teaching, my local friendships, my visits to Mother in Raleigh, and an occasional trip connected with my writing (I'd begun to get invitations to read at colleges and for various civic lecture series). Otherwise I settled into my familiar Durham life of infrequently interrupted chastity, and in the spring of '63 these stories were published in the United States and Britain to generally good reviews and the usual modest short-story sales.

There were shadowy indications that, with John Updike and Philip Roth, I was becoming one of a trio of young American writers who could be looked upon—in reviews and articles—as the Class of '32–'33. Updike was older than me by a few months, I was a few months older than Roth, and none of us had actually fought in a war. Our war proved to be the experience of our middle-class parents in the worst years of the Great Depression, years and realities that were steadily transmitted to the three of us from our earliest childhoods and about which we each wrote a good deal. I was born in February '33, the worst single month of the Depression, and thus may have written more about that awful phenomenon than my colleagues. In any case Updike and Roth sold more copies and were critically more attended to than I; but without ever being close friends, the three of us retained a sense of chronological closeness (and Roth and I have maintained a closer relation).

Before I'd decided upon a subject for my second novel, the country—in fact, the Western world, if not more—was confronted by the assassination of John Kennedy on Friday, November 22, 1963. Most everyone of my generation recalls the exact circumstances of their first awareness of the young president's murder. I was walking through a warm bright afternoon air, across the short distance from my office on to my freshman writing class in the nearby Carr Building. As I reached the outskirts of the building, I saw two of my students (one of whom was Josephine Humphreys) standing stock still, listening with grim faces to a small transistor radio.

When I approached and asked them what was urgent, they said that President Kennedy had just been shot in Dallas. We stood a few moments longer—apparently he was still alive—before I said that we should climb to our classroom and continue listening. We'd all gathered in the room; and several more radios augmented the original sound, when the commentator suddenly ceased talking; and the second movement of Beethoven's *Eroica* symphony began to play—the solemn funeral march movement. After a few moments I said to the students "Then he's dead." They all looked shocked at my assumption and I told them that the same music had been played when we learned of President Roosevelt's death in 1945.

My guess was confirmed when Roger Mudd returned to the air and said that a priest had just come out of the emergency room, said that he'd administered last rites, and that the president had died. We all sat a few minutes longer, hoping some mistake had somehow been made (as one so often does at such hard times)—maybe the priest was misinformed. But no. Reluctantly, I told the students that we'd not continue meeting that day. They slowly departed and I— who still didn't possess a television set at home—drove quickly a few blocks to the house of a student friend who had a good set.

He and I sat and listened—rapt—till well into the night; then my brother, Bill, and I went to Mother's during the weekend and saw the Sunday-morning live murder of Kennedy's killer, Lee

Harvey Oswald, inside the Dallas Police Station at the incredibly unblocked hands of a strip-club proprietor named Jack Ruby. There can have been no other similarly burdened time in American history since Lincoln's assassination on April 14, 1865 and the shooting of his assassin, John Wilkes Booth, twelve days later. Franklin Roosevelt's unexpected death from a cerebral hemorrhage, after more than twelve years in the White House, had stunned the country toward the end of the Second War. Unimaginably, young John Kennedy's public murder and imposing funeral in Washington and Arlington — in the presence of his beautiful wife and two children — sank the nation into a period of mourning and bafflement unlike any prior event in my own life, and I responded like so many of my countrymen.

Since I failed at the effort to begin a second novel in Oxford, I'd clung to the idea — a complex family story that I ultimately achieved more than a decade later in *The Surface of Earth* — and I'd hoped that it would spring to workable shape soon after the publication of my short stories (more than one of my books seems literally to have sprung to life, coming to my conscious mind after apparent long marination elsewhere in my brain). But the Kennedy disaster, with my simultaneous balked effort at a love relation, marooned me in weeks of winter idleness that had me more discouraged about my future than I'd been even in my lowest days in the cold mists of Oxford.

Somehow, though, I recalled an article that Bill Blackburn had sent me during my first Oxford stint. It recounted the epic — and comic — true story of a large python that had escaped from a small carnival in North Carolina and was ultimately found and recaptured. And reading the story again, I began to think I could convert it into a comic novel which would center on the Mustian family (pronounced MUS-chun — a Warren County farm family who'd peopled *A Long and Happy Life*) and which, not at all incidentally, might cheer me on through my melancholia. Despite the fact that I have bales of preliminary notes, over several years, for the story that became my first novel, I have only a very few pages of speculations for this second long story. I know, however, that I worked on it fairly rapidly (for me) and that—at a time when I was involved in more than one sexual adventure, as well as the Kennedy sadness— its comedy and its picture of a sexually maturing boy, surrounded as he was by a caring family, went a considerable distance toward maintaining my hold on sanity.

The other force that curbed my tendencies toward chaos at the time was a gathering mystery in my mother's life. Not long after I'd settled back into my small cubes of space by the rural pond and woods, she began to sense a dimming of vision in both her eyes. In the year I'd been away, she turned fifty-seven years old and was still holding down her full-time job in the boys' clothing store. More and more, the long hours of standing on her feet in retail sales had begun to tire her; and increasingly in the years since Dad's death, she'd been subject to unpredictable but intensely painful bouts of trigeminal neuralgia or, as it's often called, *tic douloureux* (pronounced "tick dolly-rue" in our part of the world). One of her paternal uncles, William Pryor Rodwell—who was born in 1855 but whom I remember quite clearly—suffered the same affliction, and he apparently described the symptoms as identical to those in Mother's later experience.

The trigeminal nerve moves across the sides of the human face in branches, up toward the eye and down toward the nose and lips; and the various triggers for assaults of pain remain frequently mysterious. Sometimes Mother would be free for weeks, even months, from the torment; but her attacks generally lasted for hours—often a whole night (the pain was almost always nocturnal). In the years

Elizabeth Price with her son Bill at his graduation from Duke in 1963. She had recently endured a painful procedure at Duke Hospital that detected two cranial aneurysms. Her wary eyes hint at her dread of impending surgery. Less than two years later, one of the aneurysms ("time bombs" as she called them) exploded and killed her. Reynolds was the photographer, and this image was among his favorites.

of her neuralgia there was almost no known drug available for reliable help. In fact, her only medical relief came from direct injections of alcohol into one of the branches of the nerve, especially that just above the upper lip. But that relief would last only a few days or weeks; and her several neurologists in Raleigh would speculate about the wisdom of dissecting the nerve at its root, but they'd mostly add that patients who underwent the surgery often got only temporary relief—the nerve, like so many offended nerves, had a dreadful memory. So I could never bring myself to urge Mother in the direction of surgery, and relief ultimately came from the discovery of a cause for what seemed her initially unrelated loss of vision.

The loss was so rapid and great, however, that a few months after my return home, she was compelled to resign her job (with the understanding that she might return if the blindness could be reversed). She missed some of the social aspects of her work but was never at a loss for friendship, and she never surrendered her treasured driver's license. No ophthalmologist was able to give her glasses that helped nor to detect, by peering into the inner eyeball, any visible problem that might be corrected by surgery.

After we'd exhausted the medical resources of Raleigh and a locally famous eye clinic in Durham, I took her to the neurology department at Duke Hospital (why we waited so long to go to Duke—my employer—I'm not sure, perhaps because Mother resisted the notion of going to so large a center, the place so many of our relations and friends had gone for heart and cancer problems that proved incurable). In fact in her first few days there, conventional X-rays showed no cause for her blindness; MRIs had not yet appeared in the States and would not for nearly two more decades. A psychiatrist even visited her to investigate the possibility that the cause of her trouble was psychic; but on perhaps the fifth day at

Duke, she underwent a process that was unforgivably painful for her (who'd borne so much lifelong pain stoically)—the injection of a contrast medium into certain of her cervical nerves. She responded with near-seizures and nausea, but the culprits were at last discovered—and there were two of them.

When she was wheeled back to her room from those final tests, I met her at the door and with glad sobs she said "Son, they know what it *is* now." She was no more than a few feet past me, when her Duke neurologist—Dr. John Pfeiffer, a man notorious for his hobnail-booted tactlessness—said, loudly and clearly, to me "Yes, and it's the worst thing it could possibly be."

She'd finally been discovered to have two sizable aneurysms on arteries that lay on either side of the optic chiasm, the site where the optic nerves (coming out of the back of each eyeball) meet and proceed into the brain. The chance of there being two simultaneous aneurysms in those particular locations was phenomenally unlikely and treating them surgically was going to be a stiff challenge to her surgeon.

That man was Dr. Guy Odom, famous among the Duke Hospital staff for his outrageous language in the operating room and his lack of patience with the slightest professional carelessness but noted as well for his preternatural skill. With Mother, however, he was gentle and warm, sitting on the foot of her bed and telling her what her lengthy surgery (in June of '63) had managed to accomplish. Apparently, aneurysm treatment had not progressed to its present level of frequent success; and with Mother, Dr. Odom managed to insert a device much used then in dealing with cranial aneurysms— a Crutchfield clamp that reduced the pressure in one of her aneurysms to a considerably less threatening degree.

The other ballooned artery proved impossible to defuse; and Dr. Odom eventually explained to Mother—in his kindest manner—

that the undealt-with aneurysm might accompany her unproblem-
atically for many more years. Or it might rupture at any point and
result in rapid unconsciousness and death. I don't think Dr. Odom
introduced the phrase into his conversations with her, but somehow
Mother decided to describe her problem as a "time bomb" in one
of her arteries. To cheer her, Odom predicted that—as the result of
the more successful half of the surgery—she'd almost surely recover
a great deal of her lost vision over the next eighteen months.

And in fact she did. When she returned to our Raleigh home,
her three sisters came down from Warren County and stayed with
her for some two weeks, helping with household chores that they
considered difficult for her. When I'd speak with her alone, though,
she said that—while grateful for their intention—she was a little
exhausted with their concern and much looked forward to being
alone again. Truthfully, she did need considerable initial help; and
I was glad for my aunts' presence with her.

I was maybe still oppressed by my memory of what she'd told
me, quite simply and without tears, the night she learned of her two
aneurysms. When I tried to cheer her with a little encouragement
(which I knew to be exaggerated), she listened politely; then said
"Yes, Son, but all my life I've been the Jonah." I'd never known her
to reveal special knowledge of the Bible, but her unadorned sentence revealed baldly her knowledge of the Old Testament Book
of Jonah—how his shipmates cast Jonah overboard in a powerful
storm in the hopes of calming the sea. Not at all incidentally, at
that time Jonah is fleeing from a command of God's that he go to
Nineveh and denounce the wicked inhabitants. In the sea, Jonah
is promptly swallowed by "a great fish," commonly called a whale.
I didn't probe the specifics of Mother's identification with Jonah;
what I heard, though, was her deep sense, previously unspoken (to
me in any case), of being someone repeatedly thrown overboard

Elizabeth Price, smoothing her hair, with her three older Rodwell sisters: a seated Ida Drake, Louise Rowan, and Alice Britton ("Britsy") Rodwell (Britsy had married a second cousin). This photo was taken in Macon, North Carolina in the early 1940s in front of the house built by their father six decades earlier. Elizabeth stands apart from her sisters' loose triangle (even her dress and shoes declare her separation). She loved them (especially Ida), but the death of Elizabeth's parents before she was fifteen gave her an orphan's suspicion and stubborn independence.

in a storm. Like Jonah, she was somehow a propitiatory sacrifice—abandoned to spare the others among us. I realized at once that she had been just that, and I made no attempt to counter her claim. Among her misfortunes, both her parents had died in her childhood, she'd married a lovable yet nonetheless alcoholic man who took the whole first decade of their marriage to achieve sobriety, she lost the second child she conceived and all but died in the process, and her husband died before she reached the age of fifty.

Dr. Odom was right. She recovered, in under a year, virtually all the vision she'd lost. But when she returned to Duke after that year to have her surviving aneurysm checked, she underwent the same dye study X-rays and again responded with violent tremors and nausea. The aneurysm was indeed still there, as before; and when I drove her home to Raleigh at the end of a two-day hospital stay, she calmly told me she'd never repeat those exploratory tests—please never ask that much of her again. I promised her I wouldn't, and she lived on through another whole year in relative peace. She'd never had to surrender her driver's license (something that had been a major dread for her), she'd continued being able to visit her local friends and even to drive as far, on her own, as the sixty-odd miles to Warren County to visit her home place in Macon and her beloved sister Ida who'd reared her when their parents died.

Occasionally there'd be a mishap—once she knocked down a line of yellow plastic markers before she saw them (no real harm done), and once at night she collided with another car's bumper in maneuvering out of a tight parking place (she left the scene of that accident without stopping; a benign policeman witnessed the event, followed her home, and calmly gave her a ticket for which she paid a small sum in court a few weeks later). She'd clearly never have got her license renewed at the next four-year interval. But she hurt no human beings or animals in the interim; and since the driving kept her healthier than she might have been, cooped up at home, I made no attempt to discourage her rolling onward.

And in some ways, I think her final eighteen months were among the happiest of her life. She saw the friends and kin she valued most, she had almost no worries about the condition of her house or even her clothing. (More than once, I offered to buy her new skirts and jackets; but she always declined. She finally said "I'm clean and these clothes aren't showing bare spots or holes, are they?" At a glance, I could see none and retired from that particular field.) At civil intervals after her death, I received surprisingly large bills from her insurance agent and the owner of her gas station. Both men said she was such a funny lady, they'd carried her debts with no great concern, knowing she'd eventually make them good. She never revealed the debts to me and showed me no signs of worry in the matter, and I made her word good once she was gone.

Even her death in 1965 seemed easy. Two years after her surgery, she was sitting with a neighbor in the den at her home. Upstairs, one of her favorite nephews was in bed with heart trouble (he'd come back with her from her latest trip to Macon); and she was on the telephone to his doctor. Suddenly she looked up to the neighbor, said the customary sentence at the start of such calamities—"I've got the most awful pain in my head"—then dropped the phone and slumped in her chair. The neighbor eased her down to the floor, tried to speak with her but got no initial response, though Mother's eyes were open. Then she lightly pressed the friend's hand in reply to a question—"Are you still in pain?"—and never replied to anyone else, not aboveground in this world at least.

The neighbor phoned me to say my mother had just gone to Wake Hospital in the ambulance. At that moment I was leaving my house to give a reading in Chapel Hill; my hand was literally on the doorknob to leave when the telephone rang. At first I thought I'd ignore the call, but something made me turn and answer. When I heard the news, I had one sensible thought amid confusion—I should call a friend to come drive me to Raleigh; I might well be too anxious to drive safely. The first friend I dialed was not at home; the second friend—a student in Chapel Hill named John Atkins—answered and came at once to help me.

When I reached her hospital room, her doctor happened to be there, standing beside her. Mother was lying flat on the bed, eyes shut. Though she wasn't moving with visible breaths, I somehow knew she couldn't be dead. The doctor told me her aneurysm had ruptured more than an hour ago and that the damage to her brain was already so severe she could almost surely never regain consciousness. Did I wish them to connect her to life-sustaining equipment? I asked him to talk with me about that.

In essence, he said that they could now connect Mother to machines that might keep her alive for another twenty years; but that he was convinced she'd never recover consciousness. She could only lie on in this present vegetative state.

I told him I'd never wish such a fate on Elizabeth Price.

He took a long moment to examine my face closely (though he'd been Mother's personal physician for several years, this was the first time I'd met him). Then he said "I was hoping you'd say that—" We were still some years away from widespread commitment to such a concept as living wills, directions as to how our lives might be managed in the event of our inability to make our wishes clear.

Since his pause seemed to be asking for unmistakable confirmation, I said something like "Well, I've said it then. I think we should let her present condition develop itself." I knew that my brother was, at present, on a ship in the Caribbean and reachable only with considerable slowness. I also felt certain of his agreement with my feeling (by the time I answered the doctor's implicit question, I'd been in Mother's room for no more than two minutes). I was in a state of shock that I still remember. Despite the fact that I'd loved her unquestionably more, and longer, than anyone else in my life, I'd just instructed her doctor (with no sense of doubt)—in the odd courtly code we were using to communicate—to permit this body that had made my body more than thirty years ago, and had since dealt with me in boundless generosity, to rush ahead and die.

The doctor nodded, spoke quietly with a nurse behind me, then left. I stepped to the bed, touched Mother's cool right hand, then reached a few inches onward and slipped from her left hand the wedding ring that had been there since she and Dad married in Portsmouth, Virginia in 1927. I bent and kissed the deeply furrowed brow, then went out and asked John Atkins to take me to our house on Byrd Street.

When we got there, Pia—who'd married Bill in December 1964—had just arrived. My message had somehow reached her in the theatre in Durham where she and her own mother were watching a Disney film. Because I suspected that we'd hear from the doctor in the course of the night, I decided to spend the night in Raleigh; and John Atkins and Pia chose to stay with me. I have no memories of the evening itself, though I know that when the upstairs hall phone rang at four in the morning, I went out to answer; and while I was speaking with her doctor, Pia and John also joined me in the hall—Mother had died a short while ago, never having rallied or opened her eyes. The three of us went downstairs, made coffee, and sat—mainly in silence—till I knew I must speak with a funeral director and make plans to have Mother's body collected from the hospital morgue.

Later in the morning, a representative of Brown's in Raleigh, the same firm that handled Dad's funeral eleven years earlier, came to the house. A youngish man sat with me in the den and allowed me to give him what I knew Bill and I would agree was required in the way of guidelines. The funeral would be at her church—Edenton Street Methodist in Raleigh—and burial would be beside Dad in the plot he'd bought in Oakwood Cemetery not long before his own death. The man from Brown's asked me one last question—would the coffin be kept open when it came to the house? I said No, only if my brother wished to see Mother, assuming he could get back in time for the funeral. Nonetheless, I told the man that no makeup should be applied to Mother's face, only her short hair would be simply combed. The young man was seated on a footstool near me. Now he leaned forward and tapped me on my trick knee, which promptly gave a kick. Then he locked on my eyes and said with such fervor that I felt he'd waited half his life to say it—"Oh Mr. Price, we don't *doll* 'em up."

It took Pia two days to contact Bill through the Red Cross; and it eventually proved that he would have to be transferred from his own ship which was then in the Caribbean to another ship, heading for Norfolk, and thence by plane to Raleigh. The funeral then would be postponed longer than the usual two or three days to await his return. Meanwhile, I proceeded with the dozens of other arrangements—the many calls to family and friends, booking the church service and requesting the music from the organist (the same two pieces, both by Bach, that had been played at Dad's service—"Jesu, Joy of Man's Desiring" and "Sheep May Safely Graze"), the digging of the grave at Oakwood, and (most pleasingly to Mother, if she could have known), the contact with our old housekeeper Bessie Williams in Warrenton and Bessie's agreement to spend several days with us in Raleigh, helping with the company and the arrival of quantities of ready-cooked food, a custom as old as the Anglo/Black South itself and likely as old as funerals.

The ticking off of arrangements from my list was one more

attention-collector that helped me postpone real confrontation with the large fact among us—Elizabeth Martin Rodwell Price's departure. It was only with the arrival in Raleigh of Mother's chronologically nearest sister, Alice Britton or Britsy, that I finally gave in. For some reason she and I were upstairs in Bill's old bedroom with the door shut, talking, and I suddenly broke into tears, for the first time. I'd been sitting on Bill's bed; now I lay down across it and gave in to hard weeping. Aunt Ida had been the sister who reared Mother at their parents' death, but Britsy was only five years older; and while her punctilious attention to duties often wore on Mother's nerves, there was never any doubt of their mutual devotion.

She sat beside me on Bill's narrow bed, then laid a single hand on my back, and said "Let it out, Son. Let it all out." Britsy had two grown daughters, no son; but her husband had died recently of heart trouble, and she knew the full pain of profound loss. I was old enough to have a near-total awareness of all I'd lost here, and this statement of shared grief from an aunt not given to personal revelation went some distance toward letting me do just what she said— "Let it all out." It would be a lifetime, of course, before the balance of the weight of my whole loss could be partially diminished; but at least I helped myself a good deal, then and there, for now with tears that honored her life and the pain of her death.

Bill reached home in helpful shape and felt no need to open the coffin for a final look. After the funeral, on a bright May afternoon—and knowing that my brother would be headed back to his ship in a day or so—I suggested one chore we might accomplish before he left. Having just bought a house four months before, and possessing almost no chairs and tables to furnish it, I suggested that he and I move through the house for several minutes and discuss our inheritance. Mother had left a holograph will, on a short piece of paper, making her two sons the sole heirs and joint executors of her estate; but she hadn't specified which of us got what in the way of our dozen or so pieces of good family furniture.

Given that Bill and I had never had the slightest serious disagreement about any important matter, I suggested the following plain solution for the apportionment of good pieces—we'd point to a particular item and ask whether each of us was interested in taking it. If both of us said Yes, then we'd simply flip a coin; and the winner would get the piece. Thus we proceeded through an early-nineteenth-century sideboard, an old McCraw family walnut dinner table, a couple of marble-topped washstands, a sofa and several chairs, etc. At the end of twenty minutes of flipping, we'd each acquired almost every piece he wanted; and succeeding years have revealed no dissatisfaction with our simple method. A friend with a pickup truck soon brought my pieces to my cavernously empty new home; Bill's pieces stayed in Raleigh, awaiting our decision on a possible sale of the house.

In the few more days before Bill returned to his ship, we spent a good deal of time together, discussing urgent family matters. First, we decided that—since neither of us could foresee living in Raleigh again and that the family home needed a good many repairs which Mother had kept postponing—we'd soon seek out a sympathetic Realtor and put 2311 Byrd Street up for sale. We further decided that Pia and I would devote considerable time in the coming weeks toward meeting in Raleigh and going together through Mother's mountainous private papers and other documents, discarding the discardable, then making amicable choices involving lesser physical objects that seemed (for whatever practical or sentimental reasons) worth saving. Finally we'd sell off the numerous tables, chairs, rugs, lamps, and kitchen appliances that neither of us wanted. By the time we'd seen Bill back off to his ship, we'd managed to crowd his leave-time with enough domestic business and family gatherings to bridge temporarily whatever emotional chasms might await us.

So the summer of 1965 advanced. We'd never had air-conditioning in the Raleigh house, not even a window unit; and the summer swelter affected all my and Pia's plans. I had my morning work on the comic novel—ultimately *A Generous Man*—to put behind me before my conscience could tolerate the half-hour trip to Byrd Street and two or three hours of work there, with only the huge upstairs attic fan to provide a semblance of moving air. Mainly, though, I'd collect Pia; and we'd take up our agreed-upon shares of the huge job. My own first share was the paperwork. Mother had saved almost every scrap of paper that preserved the least significant record of a financial or personal transaction. Less than one percent of the cache was worth saving—and not a single page contained a revelation, cheering or depressing—but it proved impossible to discard, before scanning, a single page. Until I reached the bottom of the chore, I couldn't know that nothing here was truly important, though family letters— from Dad to Mother or the two of us boys to our parents or dozens of other communications—seemed worth sending on someday to the Duke Library's burgeoning archive of documents relating to my work and my family's life (documents that the head librarian had begun requesting not long after I began to publish books). Pia dealt with the upstairs bales of linens, towels, clothing, and books (other than my own boyhood collection, which I mostly gave to the son of family friends—a small part of which returned to me after that son's premature death).

Ultimately I discarded at least two hundred pounds of paper and saved maybe twenty. Pia sent equivalent amounts of her findings— plus a small mountain of furniture—to the Salvation Army. The city garbage department trucked off four or five loads of miscellaneous near-junk. Then at last the house was empty, a willing Realtor was found, and—in our eagerness to throttle rapidly what had become (for me at least) a painfully still-living creature—Bill and I agreed by phone to sell the only long-term family home we and our parents had ever owned for a good deal less than we'd have accepted if we'd sought calm advice.

In those dispiriting weeks there was a single revelation—an entirely unexpected piece of news that has gone on enlightening my sense of my parents through subsequent years. Mother's closest friend on our street was Mary Cowden from two houses uphill (and originally from Pennsylvania). In recent years the two women had watched a midday television quiz show together, always at Mary's house. I'd seen Mary several times in the course of our wait for Bill's arrival and then at, at last, the funeral, but it was only as I came near the end of the clean-up that Mary saw my car parked at Mother's and walked down with no warning. Pia was not with me that day, so Mary and I sat alone together in the living room.

Given Mary's weight and her difficulty in walking, it was unusual to have such a visit; and for the first few minutes of aimless talk, I couldn't imagine her purpose in being here. After our first real pause, though, she finally said "Reynolds, I've waited as long as I could to tell you one thing." Then she waited so long in silence that I began to dread whatever would come next—some piece of hard news? Finally she launched into what she'd come to bring me—an actual story. As soon as I got to Durham that evening, I typed out a quick attempt to preserve it in Mary's own words; and since I used most of that version in *Love and Work*, a novel I wrote two years later, I'm clear enough as to what she told me.

It was at midday on the afternoon of Mother's fatal hemorrhage that she told Mary something genuinely extraordinary—and so unlike my nonfantastic mother that I've always been forced to believe it. Since I worked hard to preserve Mary's original story in my novel, I'll repeat those few hundred words here, changing only my father's name (in the novel, he's called Todd).

You know how, every night, I take off my clothes about half-past-eleven and put on pajamas and lie on the couch in the den and watch TV, always Johnny Carson—and always doze off, silly fool, lying there and wake up at two or three a.m. with the empty tube there, blasting beside me. Last night I did all that—and went to sleep and woke up at two, with the set still jittering. I sat upright on the couch and shook my head and said—aloud—"Me and my foolish naps" and saw Will sitting in his chair on my right. Three feet away, as natural as you, not speaking and looking towards the door. It was any night of my life, I must have thought; so I stood up and went to the TV, switched it off and walked through the living room, dining room, to the downstairs bath and was there, on the seat, thinking "Will needs a haircut" before I knew what had happened, was happening. Twelve years. I was not afraid—that's the other sure thing; the first is, Will was there where he hadn't been for twelve years—I didn't think of being afraid. I was still as calm as any night, calmer. I got up. I took my time and walked back carefully towards the den and stopped in the door. By then, the chair was empty.

I was far from being a confirmed believer in ghosts—or the returning dead in any form; but Mary Cowden's calm in relating the story, and the fact that she'd waited several weeks to tell me, lent her narrative (and the implicit voice of my mother behind it) a credibility that survives even now, more than forty years after I first heard it. My mother believed that she had seen my father almost twelve years after his death, in some form of the flesh, roughly twenty-four hours before her own death. She apparently didn't question the normal authenticity of what she'd seen, and she likely had no idea that such a story—a long-dead loved one coming to summon a living relation to death and beyond—is one of the commonest forms of uncanny human experience (and having phrased my description carefully, I should state firmly that I make no claim for or against the reality of any such experiences). And while *A Generous Man* was still unfinished, I soon thought that somehow I'd build another novel around Mother's credible sighting of my father, whatever its nature, just hours before the cranial catastrophe that finally bore her toward him.

Mother died during the spring semester of 1965 when I was on leave from Duke. I was acting as Writer in Residence at the University of North Carolina in Chapel Hill, eight miles from Duke. My duties involved the teaching of a single writing class and office hours that made me available to any students who might drop by. Otherwise I was writing as much as I could to finish *A Generous Man*, which was then called *Clear Day*; and I was settling into the house I'd bought in January. The details of that transaction are, I think, especially relevant to the story I'm telling.

Sometime late in 1964 I'd been standing with my long-term landlord, Henry May, in his backyard—just beside my trailer-house—when he suddenly pointed to the far shore of his pond and said "Wasn't that a pity about Mrs. Addison?" I'd never heard of Mrs. Addison but learned that she was the wife and mother in a family who'd built a house on the far pond bank three years ago and then been killed in a car wreck just a few days ago. When Mr. May went on to tell me that her husband and two young daughters had moved out of the house immediately after the funeral, an idea struck me. That night I phoned Mr. Addison, introduced myself, and said that if he was thinking of selling the house, I'd be very interested in knowing some details.

Vance Addison proceeded to tell me that he and the girls were living in a rented house now and were understandably uncertain of their plans. He'd keep me in mind if he did decide to sell. Meanwhile he told me where he'd concealed a key. If I'd like to go in and see the place, I could do so. I took his offer the next afternoon and liked the conventional redbrick and timber ranch house of the 1960s—three bedrooms, two baths, a living room, kitchen, front hall, downstairs den and laundry room—all on three levels. In another call to Addison that night I reiterated my interest. In a few more days he called me to say that yes, the property was for sale—$25,000 for the house and two-acre lot. I told him I'd make financial inquiries immediately and let him know.

Next morning I phoned Diarmuid Russell in New York and asked whether the offer to write a screenplay of A *Long and Happy Life* for Jack Garfein, the director, was still available to me. Fred Coe's option had recently lapsed, and Garfein—who was then married to the successful young actress Carroll Baker, star of the scandalously successful Elia Kazan 1962 film of Tennessee Williams's *Baby Doll*—had stepped forward to fill the gap. Through Diarmuid, I'd told Garfein that I still had no interest in the job; but now perhaps I did. Diarmuid phoned me back late that day to say that the offer was still open, and I'd be paid $25,000 for a first draft and a set of changes. Could it be a coincidence that the two sums on the table were identical and that I'd both liked the Addisons' property and been strongly drawn to the notion of continuing to live a few hundred yards from where I'd been, except for the year in England, since the fall of '58—an almost new country house on a red-dirt road some quarter hour from Duke's campus?

In short, I spoke with Jack Garfein by phone (I'd recently liked his first film, *The Strange One*) and learned that he'd like me to produce a first draft, then come to Los Angeles and discuss possible changes. I agreed, Diarmuid vetted the relevant documents before I signed; and then he sent me the first check—half my eventual pay, a handy $12,500. I went to a Hillsborough savings and loan eight miles due west, the present holders of the mortgage on the house, satisfied their concerns, made a fifty percent down-payment on the property, moved in with my few boxes of clothes, books, pictures, a dining/writing table, two chairs, and a few pots and pans. Then I began work on my screenplay.

So my new home, which I acquired in January '65 and am still occupying (more than forty years later), has been far and away the most stable of the homes of Will and Elizabeth Price's elder son. Mother and Dad had built a small house in Dogwood Acres, outside Asheboro, N.C. in 1938 when I was five and still their only child. We lived there some three years, then were forced to sell out (though I wasn't told at the time, the mortgage payments had proved beyond Dad's power to meet on a regular basis—he sold electric appliances door to door in a Depression-era mill town). We lived back in the city limits for another three years—the happiest of my childhood, what with learning to play touch football and progress rapidly up the ranks of the Cub Scouts, acquiring numerous friends as I likewise progressed through the only grades available in Park Street School—grades one through five. Then—for me—relative disaster struck.

Dad, who'd been paid so skimpily at Carolina Power and Light Company, was suddenly offered a good deal better job managing a new appliance department for the Farmers Cooperative Exchange. Since steady traveling would be involved through central Carolina and southern Virginia, he could choose to live almost anywhere along the way. He and Mother settled on life back in Warren County, their (and my) birthplace. All three of Mother's sisters lived there, as did Dad's three sisters and almost all his close boyhood friends. In retrospect, I'm sure he really made the choice of a return to the family roots, neglecting to realize that—in movement-crazed America—even a county that seemed as frozen in time as Warren County had altered significantly in the decade since we'd left. His hopes for a welcome back to our extended family were seriously deluded; even Mother's sisters (less rivalrous than Dad's) were not an ideal harbor. And I, who'd lived nowhere that I remembered nearly so happily as Asheboro, was deeply disturbed at the thought of leaving literally all the friends I had on Earth. The first prayers I ever remember making in earnest all but demanded that God keep us in Asheboro.

He didn't and I underwent a fair amount of adolescent misery in Warrenton. The point of this digression, however, is to say that—after our brief ownership of a house in Asheboro—our family never owned another of our numerous residences till we moved to Raleigh in 1947.

It's one of my pleasures in the house I bought and still own that Mother was very much alive when I moved in and that she spent at least five nights under my roof before she died some four months later. (I can't remember whether she cooked a meal here, though she was what she called "a pretty good short-order cook." On one indelible occasion, though, in the midst of a cold midwinter night, my furnace broke down; and the house quickly began to go chilly. Mother came into my bedroom and woke me with the news, whispering as though there were crowds of listeners. Knowing that no other solution was immediately possible, I rolled aside and made room for her to lie next to me under my several blankets—our last night together.) That silent nearness was close to the best gift she ever gave me, apart from thirty-two unbroken years of thoughtful care she gave my whole life up till her death—and has gone on giving: perpetual Jonah though she knew herself to be, always paddling at the outside edge of a boat that desperately tried to escape her rescue.

So the house has been the single best purchase I've yet made — the house and the forty-odd acres of rolling woods and pasture I eventually banked around it. On the night I moved in, my brother's Italian father-in-law — Pietro Tavernise, a native of Sorrento — knocked on the front door and, while he wouldn't enter, handed me another useful gift. In the three years I'd known him, he'd come to call me "Rinaldo Ribaldo," my favorite of the nicknames hung on me by friends. As he handed me a small brown bag he merely said "Ribaldo, this is what good Sorrentini give each other when they make fresh moves." Alone again, I opened the bag and found half a loaf of newly baked bread, a big pinch of sea salt wrapped in foil, and a note in lucid Italian script. I've long since lost the note and consumed the gifts, but I know I was told that the bread and salt were meant to be the start of a helpful long life. I won't speak to my degree of helpfulness; but I've already mentioned how much longer I've lived than either of my parents or my mother's parents for that distant matter (they died in their forties before I was born).

My pleasure in the unfamiliar satisfaction of suddenly becoming a "man of property" did not curb the force of a tall wave of sadness that swept down over me when I'd finally surrendered my keys to Mother's house and turned to arranging my share of her furnishings at my new address, which despite hundreds of trees was Chapel Hill township. But describing the full nature of my sadness must await the completion of the screenplay I'd signed for, my first work in Hollywood.

Most of the work was in fact done in my old house-trailer and the freshly painted house I'd bought. In the early days of my success with

A *Long and Happy Life*, I'd firmly resisted all invitations to return to my story of Rosacoke and Wesley and reimagine their actions and feelings in dramatic scenes that could be rewardingly filmed. When I declined Fred Coe's offer he turned to Charles Eastman, a California writer whose script for Robert Redford, *Little Fauss and Big Halsy*, would be filmed in 1970 to considerable success.

I had no communication with Eastman as he worked—and only met him nearly twenty years later in '92 when I went to Los Angeles on a book tour—but I read his first draft; and given his slender knowledge of rural Carolina, I thought he had the beginnings of a fair enough job (I don't recall conveying my reactions to anyone). But any interest in Eastman's script seemed to vanish when Coe's option ended. In the next few years, there were rumors that Warren Beatty was interested in Eastman's script. But when Jack Garfein's interest surfaced, with financial backing from Joseph Levine, I was approached again about starting from scratch. My initial refusal was simple—I'd spent more than two years thinking and writing obsessively about a large cast of characters, and I really didn't want to turn back to them now and attempt what Chesterton called "playing the Venus de Milo on a trombone."

Only when I needed the money to buy a house did my reluctance fold. My memory of the succeeding chronology is uncertain in parts; this is a likely sketch, however. I recall that Garfein came to Durham for our first meeting in early '65. It went well enough; his enthusiasm seemed real, though hardly sky-high. I wondered aloud if he thought of Rosacoke as a role for his wife; at once he said Yes. I didn't express my own concern that she might now be old for the part (Carroll Baker was now two years older than I, about thirty-one years old to Rosacoke's early twenties); but with no question from me, Jack claimed rather convincingly that she could easily look Rosa's age. As for any ideas that he offered me on our first meeting,

I can recall only one, a fruitful suggestion. We might well wish to begin the film a few minutes before the novel begins—that is, with Rosa's family in the yard at their home. Most of her kin are headed straight for their church picnic by a nearby lake; Rosa is waiting for Wesley to come and take her, on his motorcycle, to the funeral of her black friend Mildred. With such a scene, Jack pointed out, I could show the audience who all the main characters are in relation to one another and establish the natures of more than one of them. That tip alone, elementary as it still seems, went a long way toward helping me see how I could invent material, out-of-whole-cloth scenes which were not in the novel but could be thoroughly useful for the narrative and emotional needs of a film.

I completed my first draft in time for a Christmas flight to Los Angeles. As we were an hour from our final landing, the pilot came on the loudspeaker and told us that the L.A. airport was fogged in and that we'd land in Las Vegas, be put up there for the remainder of the night, and depart in the morning once L.A. had cleared. Since I'd never visited Vegas, I was hardly disappointed in the delay. Once I'd checked into whatever large hotel was provided, I decided that— since I'd likely not return here ever—I might as well wander for a while and see what was to be seen. The center of town was hardly as absurdly fantastic as now; still it was bright and busy past midnight. So I could tell my mother (who was still alive then and had always been a great fan of slot machines), I pumped five dollars' worth of quarters into one such machine, failed to win a penny, and quit my gambling career on the spot. If I slept at all, I don't remember. But by midmorning I was in the L.A. airport and met at the door of my plane by a man who held up a card with my name printed large. It was the first time I'd been met in such a fashion, and it took me some minutes to realize that my driver knew nothing whatever about me or my business and was only there to deliver me to my hotel.

That proved to be the famous Beverly Hills Hotel; and while I wasn't assigned one of its famous deluxe cottages on the grounds, I had a pleasant-enough large room on a corridor near the lobby. The desk clerk had informed me that, as soon as I had a moment, I should go to the rental desk there and pick up the car reserved for me. *Ah hah! So this truly was Hollywood.* And when I'd washed my hands and gone to the rental desk my *Ah hah!* was certified. The rental clerk said "Oh yes, Mr. Price, I do have one spanking-new shrimp-colored Thunderbird on hand. Will that be sufficient?" I said I believed it would.

A quarter hour later I drove out—shrimp-colored indeed and with my top down onto unstinting sunshine—and made a first quick exploration of Beverly Hills itself. At first the town seemed—and actually was—small. The center was then a little less manicured and lacquered than now, and the sidewalks seemed uncrowded and oddly welcoming. As they'd soon prove to be. I recall that later— on Christmas Day itself, I truly believe; in any case the streets were almost bare—I was checking the windows of a men's clothing store when I became aware that another man was standing close beside me, also looking. I turned and was faced by, unquestionably, Ronald Reagan who gave me his famous smile and wished me a merry day (he was not yet governor of the state, much less president of the nation; but I'd seen him in a dozen films and knew his large face at once). I called him by name and wished him well likewise. He seemed pleased at the recognition, and we exchanged several sentences of small talk before going our separate ways.

That first day, however, I was back at the hotel in time to meet Jack Garfein for lunch. I think he took me somewhere notorious like the Brown Derby for our meal; then he led me to his office on a wide but quiet business street—there was a secretary's cubicle and then a room of Jack's own space. My memory of those days is vague now, so I may be composing ideal days out of my memories, but it seems I joined the Garfein family that evening. They lived in a pleasant house that backed against the actress Donna Reed's house—two stories of airy large rooms with nice large pictures (including several examples of Jacques Callot's etchings of the Miseries and Disasters of War, a huge kitchen, an outdoor roofed gallery of spaces for chaise lounges, and a sizable outdoor pool). We had drinks by the pool, with Carroll and Jack's two pre-adolescent children playing around us—Blanche at maybe seven and Herschel at maybe five. Then the five of us climbed into a single car and went to a good Chinese restaurant for dinner—a thoroughly relaxed (and on the part of the children, a well-behaved) occasion. Carroll was involved in the final costume fittings and makeup tests for her immediately forthcoming film about the actress Jean Harlow. Both Carroll and Jack were likable dinner partners, but that night Carroll seemed exhausted and decidedly too thin for her forthcoming role as the blond bombshell of the 1930s. We barely mentioned the existence of my first-draft screenplay.

Jack by now had his own copy, so I met him late next morning at his office and our discussions began. Initially, I could hear that Jack was not deliriously happy with my first draft, but he never said that outright. Still he gently made it clear that he and I would need to go through every one of my proposed scenes with a sharp eye for, primarily, dramatic economy and power—in short, I quickly realized that a novelist (however many thousand films he may have watched and unless given prior warning of the imminent danger) almost always finds it impossible to imagine how many words a first-class actor can dispense with by facial or body movement. Even before our progress through my draft began, I longed to explain to Jack how my characters, coming as they did from the upper American South, were much given to speech. In fact, in my story a main com-

ponent of the problem between my central male and female characters is that *he* can barely enunciate his feelings; and *she* oppresses
his best qualities by her refusal to see that his laconic behavior is an
ultimately useful and likable feature of his entire human nature.

In any case, we began from the start and proceeded—that first
day—through perhaps the two scenes: the main family in the yard
at their home, as Jack had suggested, preparing to leave for a church
picnic; then Rosa and Wesley roaring away on his motorcycle to
Mildred's funeral. It was at the end of our second day's work in
Jack's office that I began to realize that now was hardly the best
time for our work—his present involvement in Carroll's career, and
especially her problems (both minuscule and large) in her role in
the forthcoming *Harlow*, was really his main concern. In her much
later excellent autobiography, *Baby Doll*, Carroll discusses Jack's
business obsessions candidly and with a degree of post facto sym-
pathy that almost exactly coincides with my own ultimate feelings
about Jack.

My plans for this first trip to Los Angeles had included spending Christmas there. And on Christmas morning I indeed walked
down from the hotel to the Garfeins' and joined the family as the
two children opened their presents; after which we all had brunch
by the pool. It was only on a midafternoon walk round the neighbor-
hood—just Jack and I—that he gave me a full and deeply moving
account of his childhood and early youth (the following account
derives entirely from my memory of Jack's oral story to me and a
much later talk with his and Carroll's son Herschel, who is now an
admired young composer and librettist).

Born to Jewish parents in Czechoslovakia in '30, Jack's family
stayed on there as the Nazis arrived. Meanwhile they acquired
forged passports for the children—Jack and his sister (the first-
born)—hoping that the children might well get to what was then

called Palestine, though such a rescue was hardly likely for the parents themselves. Disastrously, the passports were intercepted by other users, the entire family were taken in a Nazi roundup, and all four of them were sent off to different concentration camps.

In his initial imprisonment Jack was a pre-adolescent boy. He told me that, bad as all the camp arrangements were, honesty required him to recall that he and other very young boys were entertained by the awful humiliations which the guards forced on elderly Jews— behaving like chickens for instance, cackling and flapping imaginary wings during morning roll call. After several transfers—and no sense of his parents' whereabouts—Jack stayed alive long enough to reach Auschwitz; and it was there, I believe, that one day he encountered his father in a line of new arrivals at the camp. His father managed to fall out of line long enough to recognize Jack. Before his father could say more, he was whipped back into line; and it was that night—or soon thereafter—that someone came to Jack's bunk and told him that his father had died that same day, killed perhaps by his sudden meeting with a son he'd hoped might have got to Palestine.

Surviving even Auschwitz, Jack reached America soon after his liberation at age fourteen or fifteen. In the next two decades he'd gone on to become Lee Strasberg's main assistant at the Actors' Studio, to direct plays in New York, and to begin his own film-directing. At the time of our Christmas walk, Jack was nearing his mid-thirties. In memory at least I can see the grayish tone of the light as we passed the far back side of his house, and I asked him "Do you dream about it now—those days in the camps?" We took a few steps onward and he said "All the time. But now I dream that it happens to the children and Carroll, not me." From that hour on, I felt that I had some small understanding of his hard-driven efforts to rescue Carroll's career from the frigid hands of the producer Joseph Levine and the swarm of other men and women who controlled this or that rein of the giant carriage they all were attempting to ride—Louella Parsons was one of the oddly powerful souls he seemed to dread, the aging heiress of the old empire of William Randolph Hearst and the Hollywood gossip column she continued to manage despite the depredations of age and illness that warred to sideline her.

Later in the day, in a switch of scene and sound as dramatic as any on film, Jack took me with him to a party at the nearby home of an actress then riding the heights of her own career—Natalie Wood (Carroll stayed at home with the children). The guest list was short—there seemed to be no more than twenty of us; and to my pleasant surprise, Christopher Isherwood was there with his partner Don Bachardy. After our meeting with Spender in London in '61 Christopher had published the finest book of his life—a brief novel but as nearly perfect as novels get to be, *A Single Man*. After I'd seen a disapproving review in *The New York Review of Books* by Elizabeth Hardwick, I wrote to Christopher to tell him how fine I knew it was; and I'd had a prompt note of thanks. So when I saw him and Don almost lurking at the edge of the party, I went over to them, and we talked awhile in peculiarly laconic sentences—what was I doing in California, and was my job going satisfactorily? I told them it was, and that's all I retain from my last meeting with Isherwood—other than the perhaps strange fact that he and Don seemed to stay apart, at the party, from most other guests. Was there some sense on their part, as queer men, of being decidedly separate; or am I stretching for a social explanation where none is required?

What I clearly recall from the afternoon are two things—Wood's collection of paintings by Walter Keane (actually painted in those days by his wife, Margaret Keane), the generator of large oils of children with enormously soulful eyes; and the quite genuine seeming warmth of Wood herself (her recent performance with Warren

Beatty in Elia Kazan's *Splendor in the Grass* was likely as fine as any of the prolific work she did from her childhood role in 1947 in *Miracle on 34th Street* to the time of her mysterious death by drowning in 1981).

A day or two later, I inserted an unexpected extension into my trip when all the Garfeins and I boarded a plane in Los Angeles and flew from Los Angeles to Billings, Montana. In the past year Carroll had appeared in John Ford's last Western, *Cheyenne Autumn*. She played a Quaker schoolmarm who teaches among the Cheyenne Indians when they are deported by the U.S. Government from their native land and then make a heroic walking return (like those of the Cherokee and Navajo). The modern Cheyenne actors liked Carroll and invited her to visit them on their reservation in Montana, and our trip was the return on her promise. Incidentally, in the first-class compartment of the plane, I was introduced to friends of the Garfeins—Rock Hudson and a young male companion and the actor Robert Wagner who had once been Natalie Wood's husband (and would be again, in a later remarriage). They left us at our first stop, to ski in Aspen, I believe.

Arriving in Billings near dinnertime, we spent a first night in a hotel. At dinner we were puzzled by frequent crashes from a giant gong till we at last discovered that it crashed every time a waiter flamed crêpes suzette at another table. Next morning we were met by several white and Indian men from the Eastern Cheyenne reservation and were driven onward. On the slow way we stopped at the site of the famous battle between General Custer and his cavalrymen and a mixed party of Sioux and Cheyenne on whom the foolish Custer had stumbled in late June 1876. Custer and nearly three hundred of his men were killed near the banks of the Little Bighorn River and on a bare stretch of hillside above the stream. My boyhood absorption in American Indian history was rewarmed by the

Actress Carroll Baker with Reynolds in Lame Deer, Montana. She was there
to be inducted (along with her two young children) into the Cheyenne tribe.
Carroll had recently completed a role in John Ford's *Cheyenne Autumn*. Her
husband, Jack Garfein, was the photographer; he hoped to make a film of *A
Long and Happy Life* but never got the financial backing to achieve it.

visit, and I recall the many white stones that mark the discovery of various dead Custer soldiers.

At the reservation in Lame Deer we stayed at the home of a tribal federal official, himself a full-blood Indian, John Artichoker. We'd be there for two or three days, driven round the bleak landscape—past many Cheyenne men, women, and children who looked in mostly dire straits. Once as we were riding around fairly aimlessly, Jack told Artichoker that he and Carroll would consider funding a movie theatre for the village; and Artichoker seemed interested but (I thought) with more than a hint of the doubt that any Indian might well feel about the offered largesse of any white man.

On one of the evenings in Lame Deer, the Garfeins and I and a few of the white men who worked with the tribe went to a local restaurant. Carroll and I wound up side by side at the bar, and it was only then that—with no prodding from me—she quietly volunteered that she looked forward to the role of Rosacoke and that she and Jack would do their best to make a fine film (three years earlier, she'd been in Jack's second film, *Something Wild*, a story of rape and recovery from trauma that won little praise but still seems to me a moving piece of work). Her unexpected avowal, at the bar in Lame Deer, appeased some of my concern that Jack himself was now so deeply invested in Carroll's career that he had little energy left for my script, though the matter of Carroll's age—despite her unquestioned beauty—continued its silent picking at me.

Prime among the few Cheyenne whom we actually met was John Wooden Legs, tribal president of the Northern Cheyenne from 1955 to '68. One morning he and I were left alone in the living room of the Artichokers' house, and I proceeded cautiously to ask him questions about his family. Finally he told me that his grandfather, also named Wooden Leg (in the singular, for his tireless ability to walk), had been a warrior in the Custer battle at the age of eighteen.

Then he went on to tell me several boyhood memories he had of his grandfather's stories of the battle—how, for instance, astonished the young Indians were when, toward the end of the battle, numerous white soldiers turned their weapons upon themselves rather than be taken alive. Few of those Indians apparently were even familiar with the concept of suicide; yet even in boyhood I'd heard the old cliché *In a fight with the red man, save the last bullet for yourself.*

At the time of our talk, John Wooden Legs was then in his early sixties (his grandfather had died in 1940); and while he was mostly silent and self-effacing when Carroll and Jack were present, he came into his own in the final night's celebration—a big barbecue and tribal gathering in the local schoolhouse. In addition to the good food and delicious fry bread, there was music from Indian drummers and flute players; and then Wooden Legs presided over the induction of Carroll and her children into the tribe. Having seen more than one such ceremony in jokey Pathé newsreels back home, I felt a little amused at the prospect; but Wooden Legs's solemnity as he conducted the rite was calmly impressive (as was the fact that nothing whatever was said about inducting either Jack or me into membership—only Carroll, after her connection with *Cheyenne Autumn,* and her two blood kin, Blanche and Herschel).

I flew directly home from Montana, promising to return to see Jack and Carroll in the spring. Back in the trailer-house, I turned to my plans for moving into the new house on the other side of the pond and to teaching my class in Chapel Hill and meeting with students there. I've mentioned that both experiences were likable; and through all the movement, I managed to complete work on what would be my second novel. Having called it *Clear Day,* from near the start, my editor—who in Hiram Haydn's departure was now Harry Ford—pointed out a fact that I'd already discovered with chagrin in the press.

A new musical by Burton Lane and Alan Jay Lerner was about to open on Broadway; its title was *On a Clear Day You Can See Forever*, and that lengthy clause was already being shortened to the more manageable *Clear Day*. As ever in discussions of my manuscript titles, I tried to dig in with Harry and insist on my own *Clear Day*; but soon enough I realized my folly, yielded to the inevitable, and began to search for something new and — if possible — better. By a process I can no longer recall, I settled upon *A Generous Man*. That proved acceptable to Harry, and production moved steadily forward.

My students at the University of North Carolina in Chapel Hill, though geographically fewer than ten miles from Duke, were from a good deal farther away in their psyches. Early in the second week of our work, I assigned a short prose exercise for our next meeting; and when we next gathered, I asked for their papers. Only three or four of the nearly twenty students handed anything forward; and in my astonishment I apparently conveyed a certain grave intensity which led me into a lengthy deploring of the situation.

I went on a minute or two longer than necessary; and one of the men at the back of the room eventually said, quite clearly, "Mr. Price, if you'll just relax I think you'll enjoy yourself. We're not *Duke* students." There was a silent moment while I wrestled down a quasi-volcanic need to erupt; and when at last I didn't blow, the remaining nineteen students broke into relieved laughter.

I said to the young man "You're not telling me you're not as good as Duke students surely." When he said "Oh absolutely not," the laughter renewed itself; and he went on "I'm telling you that this is *Chapel Hill*—a lot prettier place, a lot older, a lot more laid back, at least as many good writing alumni. *We'll* get the papers in eventually; and you'll like 'em a lot, I'll guarantee you." As for their writing alumni, I silently reminded myself they likely valued Thomas

Raphael ("Rafe") Jones was one of Reynolds's students in the writing class he taught at the University of North Carolina, Chapel Hill. Reynolds thought that Rafe bore a strong resemblance to the character Wesley Beavers in his first novel, *A Long and Happy Life*. His second novel, *A Generous Man*, was dedicated to Rafe.

Wolfe more than I did (we Duke alumni already had William Styron after all).

But as someone who'd availed himself often of the laid-back air of the village on the hill, its shops and restaurants, its broad green old central campus (the oldest state university in the nation) and its tree trunks way bigger than elephant legs, I quickly reckoned I should kick back indeed and wait another week or so to see what developed from these exceptionally handsome-looking men and women who were presently before me. I laughed—and reignited the room—and nearly four months of good work began to come to me from assorted Tar Heels.

(Through the years I've made no practice of saving the best of my student papers, and my memory of them inevitably vaporizes with the decades. But from that small classroom in Chapel Hill, I recall one story about a student who had sat up all night cramming for an exam; then went out into a dazzling sunrise to eat a quick breakfast before his ordeal. Then as he walks through a campus parking lot, he begins to experience the first epileptic seizure of his life. Somehow the writer subtly conveyed at least that much of a medical diagnosis to his reader; but even as the seizure drives him to his knees to grab the bumper of a cold parked car, the student thinks he's undergoing a mystic enlightenment, and he ends the tale in a radiant joy. Nearly fifty years later, I think I recall that the writer's initials were L.L. In any case, if he ever reads this, I hope he'll recontact me.)

By the time the blessed ten days of spring break arrived, I'd exhausted myself with various strands of work—*A Generous Man*; the screenplay, L.A., and Montana; teaching; and serious immersion in a love affair that I knew from the start was impossible. The other person was a few years younger and was generally agreed to be physically arresting in the unchallengeable manner of a film star like Gary Cooper. He was possessed of his own rich sense of humor;

and despite his being available for sexual intimacy between us, he was simultaneously involved with a young woman whom he meant to marry soon.

I could see how predictably uneven he might be with his male contemporaries, especially if the males conflicted with my friend's choice of the women in a room. When he was half-drunk he might be frightening in his responses to other men, yet though I was with him on many such occasions, I never once felt in the least danger from him. And when, next morning, I might mention that he'd got a little rough at last night's dinner, he'd say something on the order of "Did I cause you any worry?" I might say "Not me personally, no; but I did have a few minutes' fear for the furniture (or the china and glass)." He might laugh then and say "Well, damn the glasses; I'll buy you a dozen if there's too few left for the little you drink."

AFTERWORD

ABOUT 8:30 ON a clear Sunday morning in mid-January of 2011, my phone rang. Braden Hendricks, my brother Reynolds Price's resident assistant, was calling; Braden already had phoned 911. Reynolds's night nurse had been unable to rouse him at his requested wake-up time. She had then summoned a sleeping Braden from his upstairs bedroom. Reynolds was unresponsive and barely breathing.

I told Braden that I would meet the ambulance at Duke University Medical Center's Emergency Room. I was a half hour away in Raleigh and made it to the hospital before the ambulance did. Braden found me soon after its arrival and told me that the 911 responders had not detected a pulse in Reynolds but did note that he was still breathing. He was comatose. Reynolds never regained consciousness and died four days later on January 20.

The cause of death was a heart attack. It had occurred sometime between 4:00 a.m. (when his night nurse had helped him urinate) and a bit over four hours later when she tried to wake him for medication. His initial tests at Duke indicated brain damage as well as damage to the liver and kidneys from an interrupted blood supply. Subsequent tests showed continued loss of vital functions. When I gave the order to remove him from the ventilator shortly after noon on January 20, test results from the previous day indi-

Reynolds and I in March 1959 in Raleigh. Reynolds had begun his teaching career at Duke six months earlier (with Anne Tyler in his first class); I would enter Duke as a freshman in six months. Elizabeth Price was the photographer, and the magnolia tree behind us was in Mary Cowden's front yard. It was Mary who would tell Reynolds of Elizabeth's "visit" from Will Price the night before Mother died in 1965.

cated that he had brain stem function only. His stunning intellect was gone.

My wife, Pia, and I were joined in the Neuroscience Intensive Care Unit at Duke by the closest thing we have to a pastor, our longtime friend Maurice Ritchie, who had married us forty-six years earlier (with Reynolds as best man) and was godfather to our younger daughter, Katie. Retired from the Divinity School at Duke, Maurice still lived in Durham. I asked him to give us communion in the hospital. It was the church ritual that Reynolds valued above all others. Maurice read the Methodist communion service (the only church Reynolds or I ever belonged to was Methodist, like our mother) as Pia and I stood on either side of Reynolds's bed holding his hands while taking the bread and wine.

Soon Braden Hendricks arrived. I told him I did not want to be there when the ventilator was removed, and Braden said he would stay. I thanked him and with Pia left to go to Reynolds's house. The Duke staff had said that he would probably last an hour or so after the ventilator was removed. At about 2:00 p.m. Braden called to say that Reynolds had died. After nearly twenty-seven years of chronic pain, he was finally beyond it.

The book you have just read, which Reynolds himself titled *Midstream*, picks up where his previous memoir *Ardent Spirits* left off. He had completed 208 pages of manuscript (more than half of what he envisioned as around 350 pages) before he could no longer work because of mounting pain. His handwritten (always in green ink) notations show that the last day he made edits to his typed pages was September 6, 2010.

Early in 2009 Reynolds had begun to experience pain beyond the chronic levels he had known since 1984. He was buoyed through that spring by the enthusiastic reception of *Ardent Spirits* and made trips to Washington and New York in May for interviews and readings. But by summer, he was asking for my presence and counsel more than he had done at any time since 1986. By August he could only endure about three hours a day sitting in his wheel-chair; otherwise, he needed to lie in bed and be turned from time to time. His new resident assistant who had signed on in early July was confronting a much tougher job than he had bargained for—more nurse than companion.

By fall, Reynolds's pain became severe enough that he felt more surgery was warranted. As much as he dreaded another round of cutting on his scarred body, he saw no other option that carried the promise of more work—teaching and writing, the most important talents he could still offer to God, the world, and himself.

In mid-September, a surgeon at Duke cut through part of Reynolds's breastbone in order to reach two of his upper spinal vertebrae which had become seriously misaligned from years of being in a wheelchair and being moved about by a series of assistants from bed to chair to shower to van and on and on. After three hours of surgery, the doctor called the operation successful. He had realigned the vertebrae and secured them with titanium screws. He said that the procedure should alleviate much of Reynolds's pain, but he could not guarantee it. Reynolds had known that risk ahead of time. The bleak alternative was heightened drug therapy that would surely dull his mind.

Soon after Reynolds regained consciousness, it became appar-ent that something was wrong. He was aggressive both physically and verbally with one of his nurses in the ICU and later on with his live-in assistant. Within forty-eight hours, doctors determined that Reynolds had experienced a negative reaction to one of his medications, but the assistant had had enough. He soon resigned and understandably so. He had endured more hardship in tending to Reynolds's needs in the nearly three months of his tenure than most of the two dozen or so annual resident assistants had seen in their twelve-month runs.

Discharged from Duke after five days, Reynolds entered a convalescent center. He would be there eight days, anxious to get home the entire time. Pia, Reynolds's longtime neighbor and friend Jeff Anderson, Braden Hendricks (then a recent student of Reynolds's), a couple of past assistants who lived in Durham, and I took turns in staying with him day and night. He was so afraid of being alone for even a moment.

On Reynolds's last full day there, we had our first "hard" talk since the eve of his initial surgery for spinal cancer in 1984. I reminded him that Pia and I were now in our late sixties and neither of us had the mental or physical strength to cope with his demands at the pace we had been running for the past two weeks. Without a live-in assistant, he had to find some other source of care. We agreed that we would explore using certified nursing assistants in his home. We also talked about death.

Reynolds had always dreaded such discussions. In all our years together he initiated only one—on the day before his 1984 surgery. He told me then that I was the beneficiary of his "retirement fund" and the executor of his estate. He also said he wanted to be cremated and his ashes buried in our family plot in Raleigh alongside our parents. Now on September 29, 2009, I asked him if he still wished me to follow his earlier directive. He looked straight at me and said, "No. I want my ashes scattered on the hill behind my house, and, if possible, a small bronze plaque mounted in my backyard saying that I lived in the house nearby from 1965 until my death." He reiterated that he had a lawyer-drawn will deposited at the Orange County Courthouse in Hillsborough and that I could read it there if I wanted to. I replied that I would not.

Back in his home the next day, we started the new regimen of round-the-clock nursing assistants. That experiment was soon halted when Reynolds went back to the Duke hospital on October 5 for pulmonary embolisms. He spent nine days there during which he developed "hospital psychosis," not uncommon in older patients. Reynolds would become confused and think that he had been moved to another room, and his friends and I would not be able to find him. But the moment he entered his house on October 14, his confusion ceased. One of his physicians had told me his delusions would clear up in a week or two, but his recovery was instantaneous—literally as soon as he crossed the threshold of home.

Reynolds had begun to improve by mid-November. He attended the annual Thanksgiving dinner at my older daughter Memsy's Durham home surrounded by family and laughter. A week later, he was confident that he could teach his writing seminar at Duke beginning in early January, having hired a month before a part-time assistant to help him prepare for class and get back to work. Reynolds's voice had been weakened by the surgery. He could not project well and we joked that there was gravel in his throat. Still, he felt that with the dozen or so students in a seminar room sitting close by, things could work. As indeed they did. When class ended in May, Reynolds said that it was one of the best he had ever taught in his more than five decades at Duke.

He was also back at the computer writing regularly on *Midstream* by February 2010 and in late May attended the annual gathering of kin at a cousin's Lake Gaston home near the Rodwell homeplace in Macon where our mother and he were born. He had a grand time, and his family stories were the hit of the occasion—as in years past. When Braden Hendricks became his full-time resident assistant in mid-June, Reynolds had already begun cutting back on in-house nursing assistants and was anticipating a brief surgical procedure to strengthen his weakened voice.

Before that operation, Reynolds's pain was on the rise. His dosages of oxycontin and oxycodone were increased, and while his voice improved after the surgery in late September, an old nemesis returned. Many wheelchair and bedridden folks have frequent bladder infections, and Reynolds dealt with them off and on for two and a half decades. They invariably depressed him, and by late October he was even talking of retiring from teaching—something he had never voiced before. Teaching was not just a joy for Reynolds but a major recruiting station for hiring his next resident assistant. On November 4, he told me his pain was the worst in his long experience.

There would be two more trips to the Duke hospital trying to better him, but neither helped much. At Pia's suggestion and with the counsel of my cousin Roddy Drake, a physician who through the years helped me comprehend what the Duke doctors had said in their occasionally rapid-fire delivery, I asked that a Foley catheter be inserted for use at home rather than the disposable ones Reynolds preferred. He immediately began sleeping better, but his back pain grew unrelentingly. His Duke pain specialist tried various drug treatments to help, and by the end of 2010 had him on morphine pills which he took every six hours.

Morphine was a last resort. Reynolds had steadily opposed any medication that would dull his mind, but now he relented. Shortly after taking the drug, he would fall asleep for a couple of hours. On waking, he would often be delusional, such as the time he asked Braden: "Am I dead? Am I dead?" Braden assured him that he was alive and at home and safe. Reynolds looked around and said, "But this must be Oxford, and isn't it amazing how they brought everything for me." In that case, Braden reports that Reynolds was not anxious but rather pleased. After such episodes, as his mind cleared, he would remember the hallucination and be amused, even comforted by it. Then there would be two or three hours of lucidity (punctuated by mounting pain); the cycle then resumed as time for the next pill arrived.

Reynolds remained determined to teach his two classes at Duke in January: a large lecture/discussion on the poetry of John Milton and a writing seminar centered on the Gospels. Braden phoned me on January 6 concerned that with class due to start in a week, Reynolds was in no shape to teach. I sat with Braden and him the next day to state our concerns directly. Reynolds agreed to cancel the Milton class but believed he could handle the weekly three-hour seminar. I told him that I remained skeptical but had been proven wrong more than once in years past by his strong will to succeed. Reynolds concluded by telling Braden and me he was disappointed that the two of us had discussed this matter out of his hearing. The old lion could still bite.

The next day was January 8, a Saturday. Reynolds phoned me early and was very confused. He again thought he was at Oxford, and I told him I was on my way to visit. When I arrived about 10 a.m., I was surprised to find Matthew Spender there. Reynolds had told me that Matthew would be visiting, but I did not think he was due for another week.

Matthew is the son of Reynolds's great friend Stephen Spender. He is in many ways the physical and intellectual heir of his father. An accomplished artist and the author of a respected biography of his father-in-law, the painter Arshile Gorky, Matthew was now researching his father for another book. Stephen's decades-long correspondence with Reynolds is in the manuscripts collections of the Perkins Library at Duke, and Matthew planned to devote a week to researching it. But Reynolds was in a morphine haze when Matthew arrived, and Matthew had no prior notion of Reynolds's condition. I soon explained to him what the realities were, and Reynolds asked to see us an hour or so later. He was articulate, funny, and generous, and the three of us talked for nearly two hours. Matthew commenced a routine of daily research trips to Perkins culminating in a light supper and conversation with Reynolds about the day's discoveries. Matthew has told me that Reynolds showed no signs of pain during their meetings and was "clear in his words and polite with those who were caring for him." Since late summer of 2010, Reynolds had often said to me that he looked forward "to being Reynolds Price again." During Matthew's visits, he was.

That evening of January 8, a cousin phoned to tell me of the death of Paul Bennett, a physician married to Reynolds's dearest cousin, Marcia Drake. Paul was eighty-two and had been in poor health for years. Soon after Reynolds's initial surgery in 1984, it was the Bennetts who took him into their home in Goldsboro, North Carolina, and stayed by him through his descent into complete paralysis. Reynolds recounts their generosity in *A Whole New Life* and dedicated his novel *Good Hearts* to them. Marcia's youngest sister was the one who called me about Paul's death, and she added a bracing story. When Paul's pastor visited him in his final days, the minister told him that he would find peace in heaven. Paul responded, "It's not the destination that worries me, it's the journey." When I recounted that to Reynolds the next day, his eyes opened widely and he exclaimed, "Wow!" Then he turned his head straight at me and said, "I'm on that journey now."

January 15 was Matthew's last day, and I joined Reynolds and him that morning for stimulating conversation and much laughter. At 1:30 Matthew had to leave to get to the airport for his return home to Italy, and I saw him off in his rental car. I headed back to Reynolds's room to say goodbye since it would soon be time for his morphine dose. Reynolds smiled broadly and said, "That was really wonderful. It was almost like being with Stephen." I smiled back. "I'll see you soon, buddy." He responded, "I look forward to it." Those were our last words to each other. In less than twenty-four hours, he would have his heart attack.

Matthew Spender had given Reynolds a week of the happiest hours he had known in months. During those evening chats, Reynolds would be full of memories that pushed his pain into a corner where it did not dominate his thoughts. Having watched his daily fall into ever greater agony for months, I know that Matthew's presence was a blessing. Whatever prompted his visit, I am so very grateful for it.

On February 26, 2011, I led a small group of Reynolds's closest kin and friends up the hill behind his house to scatter his ashes. Braden bore the Jugtown Pottery urn with Reynolds's remains (or as the funeral home designated them, "cremains"—how my brother would have howled at that!). Although Reynolds, who had immersed himself in the Bible over seven decades, did not designate any readings from it, I chose two passages especially meaningful to him: Deuteronomy 30:19–20a and John 21:1–14. I also read a message from Matthew Spender describing the ease with which he and Reynolds renewed their friendship in that last full week of his life. A few members of our group shared some of their thoughts, and those who wished to do so reached into the urn with a long-handled antebellum Price family spoon to scoop and scatter ashes. Fittingly, a hawk flew right over us as we proceeded. The hill was radiating its ancient power while manifesting its name—Hawk Hill. We then walked back down to Reynolds's longest and best home, of forty-six years, and honored him with what he especially enjoyed: good food and drink punctuated by jokes and stories from folks he loved. It was one of those late February days not unfamiliar to the North Carolina piedmont—bright sunshine, clear sky, sixty degrees or so. Reynolds would have adored it all, and all of us knew it. The pleasure and good memories were palpable.

I still expect him to be in his house when I go over now to plow through his leavings; I sometimes think that the ringing phone is him calling. Eight years older, he was someone I admired and loved all my life, even in those very rare times when we argued. He was also my surest link to our dead parents and their world; that loss is profound. I miss him terribly.

Reynolds's second book was *The Names and Faces of Heroes.* He dedicated it to our parents and me. On the dedication page of the copy he gave me just before I graduated from Duke in 1963, beneath the printed "For Will, My Brother," he wrote in his strong hand, "and now more: sometimes father, sometimes son—Long love, Reynolds."

Well, Dear Old Heart, I return those words to you: my sometimes father, sometimes son. From where I sit now with a Carolina spring budding, I send you long love and every hope for peace and joy.

—William Price, March 2011

REYNOLDS PRICE
(1933–2011)

In the summer after he published A *Long and Happy Life* in 1962, and won the William Faulkner Award, Reynolds Price returned to North Carolina. He went on to publish thirty-nine full-length volumes of fiction, poetry, plays, essays, and translations, and to teach at Duke University for more than five decades.

With the profit from a never-produced screenplay, Price bought a sizable dwelling near the trailer-house where he'd completed his first books and continued to work alone in the new house, surrounded by the same trees and animals. He was likewise visited by many friends and occasional loves, none of whom proved residential. In 1984 a large malignant tumor was discovered in his spinal cord; and after radiation and four surgeries at the hands of Dr. Allan Friedman, he settled into full-time wheelchair life. The demands of a disabled existence made it necessary to add accessible quarters to his house; until his death, Price lived there with the steady help of a series of live-in assistants.

Kate Vaiden, the novel he was writing when his cancer manifested itself, was published in 1986 and won the National Book Critics Circle Award. Ensuing years saw Price publish—among numerous other books—A *Perfect Friend*, his first novel for children and adults; large collections of his short stories and poems; and a gathering of fifty-odd commentaries that he'd broadcast on National Public Radio. His time since the early 1980s included national productions of his six plays — including *Private Contentment*, a script commissioned for PBS's first season of *American Playhouse*. His dramatic trilogy *New Music*, the forty-year history of a family, premiered at the Cleveland Playhouse in a production that permitted audiences to see all three plays in a single long afternoon or on three consecutive evenings. And his *Full Moon*, originally commissioned by Duke Drama, appeared at San Francisco's American Conservatory Theater.

In 1988 he was inducted into the American Academy of Arts and Letters; his work has been translated into seventeen languages; and in the fall of 2008 he marked the fiftieth anniversary of teaching at Duke. He died on January 20, 2011.